1/02

D0604387

Discarded by
Santa Maria Library

641.822
Scheer, Cynthia.
Fresh ways with pasta
c1990

02   03   09   10

GAYLORD MG

/02

Sunset

Fresh Ways with
Pasta

By the Editors of
Sunset Books
and
Sunset Magazine

Sunset Publishing Corporation ▪ *Menlo Park, California*

For an autumn feast, serve Barbecued Quail with Pappardelle in Mushroom Sauce (recipe on page 73).

Research & Text
Cynthia Scheer

Coordinating Editor
Linda J. Selden

Design
Joe di Chiarro

Illustrations
Susan Jaekel

Photography
Victor Budnik: *59.* **Glenn Christiansen:** *31.* **Peter Christiansen:** *51.* **Tom Wyatt:** *79.* **Nikolay Zurek:** *2, 7, 10, 15, 18, 23, 26, 35, 38, 43, 46, 54, 62, 66, 71, 74, 82, 87, 90, 95.*

Photo Stylists
Susan Massey-Weil: *2, 7, 10, 15, 18, 23, 26, 35, 38, 43, 46, 54, 62, 66, 71, 74, 82, 87, 90, 95.* **Lynne B. Morrall:** *59.* **JoAnn Masaoka Van Atta:** *79.*

The Many Faces of Pasta

Tortellini, ravioli, fettuccine, pappardelle, lasagne, capellini, penne, rotelle, linguine—these are just a few of the many faces of pasta. Whether you serve it bathed in a delicate sauce for an elegant meal opener, combined with meat or poultry for a robust main course, or tossed with vegetables for a filling salad, pasta is a favorite with everybody.

Italian pasta with its repertoire of sauces is justifiably famous; our recipes present some of the best examples. But Italy doesn't have a monopoly on pasta dishes. Included in this book are recipes with international appeal, such as a Chinese-inspired won ton salad, Middle Eastern moussaka made with fettuccine, Norwegian-style meatballs and sauce served over linguine, and a Mexican version of lasagne.

As well as being versatile, pasta is also a highly nourishing source of complex carbohydrates. No matter which size, shape, or color you choose, let your favorite pasta help keep you in shape.

Special thanks go to Rebecca LaBrum for her careful editing of the manuscript and to Viki Marugg for her creative contributions to developing the art. We also thank The Best of All Worlds, Biordi Art Imports, Sue Fisher King, and Fillamento for their generosity in sharing props for use in our photographs.

For our recipes, we provide a nutritional analysis (see page 5) prepared by Hill Nutrition Associates, Inc., of Florida.

About the Recipes

All of the recipes in this book were tested and developed in the *Sunset* test kitchens.

Food and Entertaining Editor, Sunset Magazine
Jerry Anne Di Vecchio

Cover: Penne with Smoked Salmon, recipe on page 47. Design by Jean Warboy; photography by Noel Barnhurst; food styling by George Dolese; art direction by Vasken Guiragossian.

VP, Editorial Director, Sunset Books: Bob Doyle

8 9 0 QPD/QPD 9 8 7 6 5 4 3 2 1 0

Copyright © 1990, Sunset Publishing Corporation, Menlo Park, CA 94025. First edition. World rights reserved. No part of this publication may be reproduced by any mechanical, photographic, or electronic process, or in the form of a phonographic recording, nor may it be stored in a retrieval system, transmitted, or otherwise copied for public or private use without prior written permission from the publisher. Library of Congress Catalog Card Number: 89-69848. **ISBN** 0-376-02524-7

Printed in the U.S.A.

Please visit our website at www.sunsetbooks.com

Contents

Introduction 4

Soups 11

Salads 19

Vegetables & Cheese 27

Seafood 47

Poultry 55

Meats 75

Index 94

Special Features

Colorful Flavored Pastas 6

Homemade Egg Pasta 8

Pasta with Pesto 33

Great Pretenders: Vegetables as Pasta 44

Won Ton Ravioli & More 60

Polenta, Plain & Fancy 68

Creamy Pasta Pies 84

Risotto: Italian Rice 92

Introduction

The very first Italian word you ever learned may well have been "spaghetti," or perhaps "macaroni." These two favorites, along with the multitude of additional varieties you've probably encountered over the years, are collectively known as "pasta."

Though there's no doubt that Italian cooks made pasta famous, it plays a part in other national cuisines as well. In the pages that follow, you'll find not only numerous Italian specialties, but also tantalizing variations inspired by the cooking of other European cultures, Asia, and Latin America.

Pasta's popularity is easy to understand. It's fun to choose from the scores of forms, creative to dream up combinations of pasta with all sorts of sauces and dressings. And the final result is invariably wonderful to eat. Many pasta entrées can be cooked in mere minutes—and what's more, the price is usually right.

Pasta Variety

Many a good cook makes tender egg pasta at home, either by hand or with the aid of a food processor and pasta machine. If you'd like to turn out your own fresh pasta, try the Egg Pasta on page 8—and don't forget the colorful variations on page 6. You can cut any of these pastas into noodles of any width, including lasagne strips and cannelloni squares.

What if you don't have the time or desire for pasta making? Drop into a pasta shop—you'll find freshly made noodles as well as filled pastas such as ravioli and tortellini, all sold in bulk. Many supermarkets also offer a tempting variety of refrigerated packaged fresh pasta, both plain and fancy; in the freezer case, you'll come upon ravioli and their cousins—plump tortellini, lunette, anolini, and pansotti. (Look for plain, unsauced ravioli, then add your family's favorite embellishments.)

However enticing, fresh noodles and filled shapes are by no means the entire pasta picture. Dry pasta, available in myriad forms, underlies some of the most delectable dishes of all. Each kind has its special attractions — smooth cream sauces cling to curves, zesty seasonings fill hollows, rich broths invite tiny pasta bits. The selection is especially abundant in an Italian delicatessen, but any supermarket offers plenty of good options for the dry pastas specified in our recipes.

For those truly interested in exploring the vast pasta world, gourmet shops and mail-order sources offer premium-priced dry pasta in numerous shapes and a wide range of exotic flavors, from artichoke to wild mushroom.

Cooking Pasta Perfectly

By now, we've all heard that the ideal state for cooked pasta is summed up in the succinct Italian phrase *al dente*—"to the tooth," or tender but still firm. To achieve such perfectly cooked pasta, start by using plenty of water: pasta in an abundance of rapidly boiling water is unlikely to stick to itself or to the pan. Be sure to choose a cooking pan that can comfortably hold the amount of boiling water you will need.

For each 8 ounces dry pasta, bring 3 quarts water to a rapid boil. Add 1 tablespoon salt, if desired (for more pasta, increase the amount of water only). Then add the pasta to the boiling water. When you cook spaghetti or other pasta that's longer than the pan is deep, hold the bunch of pasta by one end, then gently push the other end into the boiling water until the strands soften enough to submerge. Stir only if the pasta needs to be separated. Keep the water boiling continuously and cook the pasta, uncovered, according to the cooking time specified in the recipe.

Cooking time varies with the pasta's size and shape—the thinner and moister the pasta, the shorter the cooking time. Our recipes specify the time it took our testers. But because one manufacturer's spaghetti may cook faster than another's, it's always wise to check the cooking time specified on the package. And of course, you'll want to use your own judgment. A quick, reliable test for doneness is simply to lift a piece or strand from the pan and quickly bite into it; if it's al dente, it's done. Pasta that breaks easily against the side of the pan when prodded with a spoon has probably been cooked too long.

If the pasta is destined for a baked casserole, shorten the cooking time by a few minutes to allow for additional cooking in the oven.

As soon as the pasta is al dente, drain it quickly and continue according to the recipe. Rinse cooked pasta only if you're going to use it in a salad or need to cool lasagne noodles in order to handle them. Pasta that will be served at once should not be rinsed; to keep it as hot as possible, have a warm platter or plates—and your family or guests—ready and waiting. (Don't worry about excess water clinging to the drained pasta, it will blend in with the sauce.)

How Much to Cook?

As a general rule, 2 ounces dry pasta make about 1 cup cooked pasta or 1 serving. Spaghetti and macaroni products approximately double in volume upon cooking, but packaged egg noodles don't expand quite that much. Fresh pasta is much moister than the dry product, so you'll need a greater weight for each serving—3 to 3½ ounces to make 1 cup (about 1 serving).

A kitchen scale allows you to weigh out pasta most accurately, but if you don't have one, you can measure by eye—just estimate the proportion of a package needed.

Pasta Nutrition

Pasta is low in fat and sodium; it's a good source of complex carbohydrates, and enriched pastas provide B-vitamins and iron. The durum wheat from which most pasta is made is high in protein. Finally, pasta's calorie content is lower than you may have assumed—2 ounces of uncooked spaghetti or macaroni provide less than 210 calories.

A Word about Our Nutritional Data

For our recipes, we provide a nutritional analysis stating calorie count; grams of protein, carbohydrates, and total fat; and milligrams of cholesterol and sodium. Generally, the analysis applies to a single serving, based on the number of servings given for each recipe and the amount of each ingredient. If a range is given for the number of servings and/or the amount of an ingredient, the analysis is based on an average of the figures given.

The nutritional analysis does not include optional ingredients or those for which no specific amount is stated. If an ingredient is listed with a substitution, the information was calculated using the first choice.

Added to fresh pasta dough, puréed vegetables or herbs give homemade fettuccine, tagliarini, or even lasagne eye-catching color and extra flavor. You'll find that herbs such as basil and chives contribute an especially sprightly taste.

After making any of these colorful doughs, follow the directions on page 9 for rolling and cutting by hand or using a roller-type pasta machine (the dough may be too stiff to feed through an extrusion-type machine).

All these fresh pastas cook quickly. Allow just 1 to 3 minutes—depending on the thinness of the pasta—in a generous quantity of boiling water.

Fresh Herb Pasta

Pictured on facing page

1 cup firmly packed fresh basil leaves, oregano or marjoram sprigs (woody stems removed), or coarsely chopped chives or garlic chives
1 large egg
1 tablespoon water
About 2 cups all-purpose flour

In a food processor, whirl herb of your choice with egg and water until puréed. Add 1 cup of the flour to herb purée in food processor. Whirl until dough forms a smooth, elastic ball (2 to 3 minutes). If dough feels sticky, add about 1 tablespoon more flour and whirl until blended. Wrap dough in plastic wrap and let rest for about 30 minutes. Roll and cut as directed on page 9, using additional flour as needed. Makes 8 to 10 ounces uncooked pasta (about 4 servings).

Per serving: 286 calories, 10 g protein, 56 g carbohydrates, 2 g total fat, 53 mg cholesterol, 19 mg sodium

Colorful Flavored Pastas

Red Bell Pepper Pasta

Pictured on facing page

4 large red bell peppers (about 2 lbs. *total*)
About 2½ cups all-purpose flour
1 large egg

Arrange peppers in a single layer in a 9- or 10-inch square baking pan. Bake, uncovered, in a 500° oven, turning occasionally, until skins are blackened on all sides (40 to 50 minutes). Then cover peppers with foil and let stand until cool (about 30 minutes).

Remove and discard pepper skins, stems, and seeds. Whirl peppers in a blender or food processor until puréed; pour purée into a 1- to 2-quart pan. Cook over medium heat, stirring often, until reduced to ½ cup (about 10 minutes). Let cool.

In a food processor, combine pepper purée, 2 cups of the flour, and egg. Whirl until dough forms a ball (at least 30 seconds). If dough feels sticky, add 2 tablespoons more flour; process until dough forms a ball again (at least 30 more seconds). Divide dough into 6 equal parts; wrap each in plastic wrap and let rest for at least 10 minutes.

Roll and cut as directed on page 9, using additional flour as needed. Makes about 1 pound uncooked pasta (4 to 6 servings).

Per serving: 234 calories, 8 g protein, 46 g carbohydrates, 2 g total fat, 43 mg cholesterol, 18 mg sodium

Spinach Pasta

½ of a 10-ounce package frozen chopped spinach, thawed; or about ½ cup cooked fresh spinach
2 large eggs
1½ to 2 cups all-purpose flour

Squeeze spinach dry and measure it; you need ¼ cup. In a food processor, combine spinach, eggs, and 1½ cups of the flour. Whirl until dough forms a smooth, elastic ball (1 to 2 minutes); if dough feels sticky, add more flour, 1 tablespoon at a time, and whirl until blended. Wrap dough in plastic wrap and let rest for 10 minutes.

Roll and cut as directed on page 9, using additional flour as needed. Makes about 12 to 14 ounces uncooked pasta (about 4 servings).

Per serving: 273 calories, 11 g protein, 49 g carbohydrates, 3 g total fat, 106 mg cholesterol, 59 mg sodium

Pine Nut–Butter Sauce

Pictured on facing page

½ cup (¼ lb.) butter or margarine
1 medium-size red bell pepper (about 5 oz.), seeded and thinly slivered
¼ cup pine nuts

Melt butter in a medium-size frying pan over medium heat. Add bell pepper and cook, stirring often, until limp but not brown (4 to 6 minutes). Stir in pine nuts and cook until lightly toasted (2 to 3 minutes). Makes enough sauce for about 1 pound uncooked fresh pasta (4 to 6 servings).

Per serving: 206 calories, 2 g protein, 2 g carbohydrates, 22 g total fat, 50 mg cholesterol, 188 mg sodium

*Three colors of homemade fettuccine mingle in
this bright first course. Combine equal quantities of
Fresh Herb Pasta, Red Bell Pepper Pasta, and Egg Pasta,
then drizzle with hot Pine Nut–Butter Sauce. The
recipes are on the facing page and page 8.*

Tender, springy fresh pasta dough is perfect for noodles of all sizes. To alter the flavor and texture, you can use whole wheat or semolina flour for up to half of the all-purpose flour.

Remember that the amount of liquid any flour can absorb will vary with the flour's natural moisture content and with the air temperature and humidity. In fact, you really won't know just how much water you need until you start working with the dough—so add water gradually, always paying close attention to the dough's texture.

Following we present two recipes for making egg pasta. In the first, the dough is mixed and kneaded by hand. The second recipe utilizes the food processor, which reduces mixing time to seconds and kneading time from 10 minutes to two or three. With either recipe, the dough can be rolled and cut by hand or with a pasta machine.

It's best to cook homemade pasta right away, but if you make more than you need, let it stand until dry but still pliable (30 minutes to 1 hour). Then enclose in a plastic bag; refrigerate for up to 2 days or freeze for up to 2 months. Do not thaw pasta before cooking.

The pasta-making techniques described here are also appropriate for the colorful flavored pasta doughs on page 6.

Egg Pasta

Pictured on page 7

About 2 cups all-purpose flour
2 large eggs
3 to 6 tablespoons water

Mound 2 cups of the flour on a work surface or in a large bowl and make a deep well in the center. Break eggs into well. With a fork, beat eggs lightly; then stir in 2 tablespoons of the water. Using a circular motion, begin to draw in flour from sides of well. Add 1 more tablespoon water and continue to mix until all flour is evenly moistened. If necessary, add more water, 1 tablespoon at a time. When dough becomes too stiff to stir easily, use your hands to finish mixing. Pat dough into a ball and knead a few times to help flour absorb liquid. Clean and lightly flour work surface.

If you plan to use a rolling pin, knead dough by hand: flatten dough ball slightly, then fold farthest edge toward you. With your fingertips or the heel of your hand, press and push dough away from you, sealing the fold. Rotate dough a quarter turn and continue folding-pushing motion, making a turn each time. Knead with a gentle, rhythmic motion until dough is smooth and elastic (about 10 minutes). Cover dough and let it rest for 20 minutes.

If you plan to use a pasta machine (manual or electric), first knead dough by hand, sprinkling with flour if needed, until no longer sticky (3 to 4 minutes).

With rolling pin or pasta machine, roll and cut dough by hand or by machine, as directed on facing page.

Machine-rolled dough makes about 32 pieces lasagne or about 4 cups cooked medium-wide (machine-cut) noodles (14 to 16 oz. uncooked). Yield of hand-rolled noodles may vary.

Per cup cooked pasta: 279 calories, 10 g protein, 51 g carbohydrates, 3 g total fat, 106 mg cholesterol, 33 mg sodium

Homemade Egg Pasta

Food Processor Pasta

About 2 cups all-purpose flour
2 large eggs
About ¼ cup water

Combine 2 cups of the flour and eggs in a food processor; whirl until mixture looks like cornmeal (about 5 seconds). With motor running, pour ¼ cup of the water through feed tube and whirl until dough forms a ball. Dough should be well blended but not sticky. If dough feels sticky, add a little flour and whirl to blend; if it looks crumbly, add another teaspoon or two of water. If processor begins to slow down or stop—a good indication that dough is properly mixed—turn off motor and proceed to next step.

Turn out dough onto a floured work surface and knead a few times, just until smooth.

If you plan to use a rolling pin, cover dough and let it rest for 20 minutes.

If you plan to use a pasta machine (manual or electric), you can roll dough out immediately.

With rolling pin or pasta machine, roll and cut dough as directed on facing page.

Machine-rolled dough makes about 32 pieces lasagne or about 4 cups cooked medium-wide (machine-cut) noodles (14 to 16 oz. uncooked). Yield of hand-rolled noodles may vary.

Per cup cooked pasta: 279 calories, 10 g protein, 51 g carbohydrates, 3 g total fat, 106 mg cholesterol, 33 mg sodium

Pasta by Hand

Once you've kneaded the dough and let it rest, you're ready to roll it out.

Rolling. Keeping unrolled portions of dough covered, roll out a fourth of the dough into a rectangle about 1/16 inch thick with a rolling pin. If dough is sticky, turn and flour both sides as you roll. Transfer rolled strip to a lightly floured surface or cloth and let stand, uncovered, while you roll remaining portions. Let each strip dry until it feels leathery but still pliable (5 to 10 minutes).

Cutting. Place a strip of rolled pasta dough on a lightly floured board and sprinkle with flour. Starting at narrow end, roll up jelly roll fashion and cut crosswise into slices as wide as you want the pasta. Fettuccine is about 1/4 inch wide, tagliarini about 1/8 inch wide; lasagne is about 2 inches wide.

Pasta by Machine

The following general directions apply to both manual and electric pasta machines. (Because pasta machines differ slightly in size and function depending upon the brand,

always consult the manufacturer's directions as well.)

Kneading and rolling. Keeping the unrolled portions covered, flatten a fourth of the dough slightly; flour it, then feed it through widest roller setting. Fold dough into thirds and feed it through rollers again. Repeat folding and rolling process 8 to 10 times or until dough is elastic. If dough feels at all damp or sticky, flour both sides each time it's rolled.

When dough is smooth and pliable, set rollers one notch closer together and feed dough through. Flour dough if it is damp or sticky. Repeat rolling, setting rollers closer each time, until dough is a long strip of the desired thinness. Cut strip in half crosswise for easy handling; place pieces on a lightly floured surface or cloth and let stand, uncovered, while you roll remaining portions. Let each strip dry until it feels leathery but still pliable (5 to 10 minutes).

Cutting. Feed each strip through the medium-wide blades for fettuccine or through the narrow blades for thin noodles or tagliarini. Some machines have attachments for wide and narrow lasagne, but lasagne can also be cut easily by hand.

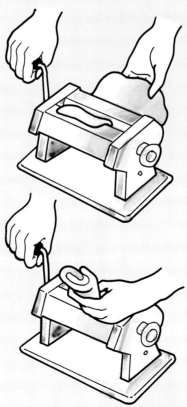

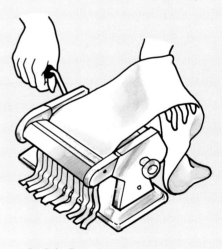

Lightly flour the cut pasta to keep strands separate. Once cut, pasta can be handled in 2 ways: you can toss it in a loose pile, or you can carefully gather the strands as they emerge from the machine (or have someone else gather them) and lay them in neat rows.

*For a cozy supper or weekend lunch, enjoy steaming
bowls of bacon-flecked Ravioli & Cabbage Soup (recipe
on facing page) and crusty bread at the fireside or
around the TV.*

10

Soups

Pasta in some form is a familiar addition to a bowl of steaming soup—golden egg noodles swirled through rich chicken broth, or an edible alphabet in disarray among the peas and carrots in a thick beef stock. Today, pasta in all shapes and sizes plays a prominent role in soups as satisfying as they are distinctive. Plump ravioli and tortellini mingle with a profusion of colorful vegetables; noodles and thin spaghetti strands lend welcome substance to light yogurt-enriched or clear broth. Tiny rice-shaped orzo, big seashells, or ruffly bow ties join hearty beans to supply cold-weather comfort.

Pictured on facing page
Ravioli & Cabbage Soup

Preparation time: About 20 minutes

Cooking time: 20 to 35 minutes

Fresh, frozen, or dry ravioli cook to plumpness in a simple bacon-seasoned broth for a nourishing lunch or supper soup.

- 4 ounces sliced bacon (about 5 slices), cut into ½-inch pieces
- 1 small onion, finely chopped
- 2 cloves garlic, minced or pressed
- 1 tablespoon chopped parsley
- 2 quarts regular-strength beef broth
- 2 cups water
- 1 large carrot (about 3 oz.), thinly sliced
- 1 pound (about 24) fresh or frozen ravioli; or 1 package (7 oz.) dry raviolini
- 2 cups shredded cabbage
  Grated Parmesan cheese

In a 5- to 6-quart pan, cook bacon over medium heat until translucent and limp. Add onion; continue to cook, stirring, until onion and bacon are lightly browned (about 5 more minutes). Discard all but 1 tablespoon of the bacon drippings; then stir garlic and parsley into bacon-onion mixture. Add broth, water, and carrot. Increase heat to high and bring to a boil. Separate any ravioli that are stuck together, then add ravioli to boiling broth. Reduce heat to medium and boil gently, uncovered, stirring occasionally, until ravioli are just tender to bite (about 10 minutes for fresh, 12 minutes for frozen, or 25 minutes for dry; or time according to package directions). Stir in cabbage during last 5 minutes of cooking. Serve with cheese to add to taste. Makes 4 to 6 servings.

Per serving: 473 calories, 20 g protein, 33 g carbohydrates, 28 g total fat, 90 mg cholesterol, 1,945 mg sodium

Tortellini Soup

Preparation time: About 25 minutes

Cooking time: About 15 minutes

Tortellini in brodo, the familiar Italian first-course soup, is transformed into a sturdy main dish when you add chicken, fresh spinach, red bell pepper, mushrooms, and rice.

      About 12 ounces spinach, rinsed well
3   **large cans (49½ oz. *each*) regular-strength chicken broth**
1   **package (9 oz.) fresh cheese-filled spinach tortellini**
1   **whole chicken breast (about 1 lb.), skinned, boned, and cut into ½-inch pieces**
8   **ounces mushrooms, sliced**
1   **medium-size red bell pepper (about 5 oz.), seeded and finely chopped**
1   **cup cooked rice**
2   **teaspoons dry tarragon**
      Salt and freshly ground pepper
      Grated Parmesan cheese

Pat spinach dry. Remove and discard stems; chop leaves coarsely and set aside.

In an 8- to 10-quart pan, bring broth to a boil over high heat. Add tortellini, return to a gentle boil, and cook, uncovered, just until tender to bite (4 to 6 minutes; or time according to package directions). Add spinach, chicken, mushrooms, bell pepper, rice, and tarragon. Return to a boil, then reduce heat so soup simmers. Cover and simmer until chicken is no longer pink in center; cut to test (about 2 minutes). Season to taste with salt and pepper. Serve with cheese to add to taste. Makes 10 to 12 servings.

Per serving: 180 calories, 15 g protein, 20 g carbohydrates, 5 g total fat, 27 mg cholesterol, 1,826 mg sodium

Tortellini

Chicken-Noodle Yogurt Soup

Preparation time: About 15 minutes

Cooking time: 30 to 35 minutes

A great warm-up on chilly days, this sprightly soup gets its pleasantly tart flavor from lowfat yogurt. Before stirring the yogurt into the soup, blend it with a little cornstarch to keep it from separating.

1   **tablespoon salad oil**
1   **large onion, finely chopped**
1   **teaspoon dry thyme leaves**
¼   **teaspoon *each* pepper and dry dill weed**
3   **cloves garlic, minced or pressed**
4   **or 5 parsley sprigs**
3   **small carrots (about 5 oz. total), thinly sliced**
2   **quarts regular-strength chicken broth**
4   **ounces dry medium-wide egg noodles**
2   **cups cubed cooked chicken or turkey**
1   **cup plain lowfat yogurt**
1   **tablespoon cornstarch**
6   **green onions (including tops), thinly sliced**

Heat oil in a 5- to 6-quart pan over medium heat; add chopped onion, thyme, pepper, and dill weed. Cook, stirring often, until onion is soft (6 to 8 minutes). Stir in garlic; then add parsley, carrots, and broth and bring to a boil. Reduce heat, cover, and boil gently until carrots are tender to bite (12 to 15 minutes).

Remove and discard parsley; increase heat to high and add noodles. Cook, uncovered, until noodles are just tender to bite (8 to 10 minutes; or time according to package directions). Add chicken.

In a medium-size bowl, smoothly blend yogurt and cornstarch. Gradually blend in about 1 cup of the hot broth mixture; then stir broth-yogurt mixture back into soup and bring to a boil, stirring. Garnish with green onions. Makes 6 servings.

Per serving: 282 calories, 22 g protein, 26 g carbohydrates, 10 g total fat, 62 mg cholesterol, 1,417 mg sodium

■ *To Microwave:* In a 4- to 5-quart microwave-safe casserole or tureen, mix oil, chopped onion, thyme, pepper, dill weed, and garlic. Microwave, covered, on **HIGH (100%)** for 6 to 8 minutes or until onion is soft, stirring twice. Stir in parsley, carrots, and ½ cup of the broth. Microwave, covered, on **HIGH (100%)** for 4 to 5 minutes or until carrots are almost tender when pierced. Remove and discard parsley; add remaining 7½ cups broth and noodles. Microwave, covered, on **HIGH (100%)** for 20 to 25 minutes or until noodles are almost tender to bite, stirring twice.

In a medium-size bowl, smoothly blend yogurt and cornstarch. Blend in 1 cup of the hot broth; stir broth-yogurt mixture and chicken into soup. Microwave, covered, on **HIGH (100%)** for 3 minutes. Let stand, covered, for 2 minutes. Stir well before serving; garnish with green onions.

Fresh Pea & Pasta Broth

Preparation time: About 10 minutes

Cooking time: About 10 minutes

Crunchy emerald sugar snap peas share the spotlight with slender strands of capellini in this light soup. Star anise and ginger flavor the broth.

- **4 ounces sugar snap peas or Chinese pea pods (also called snow or sugar peas), ends and strings removed**
- **1 large can (49½ oz.) regular-strength chicken broth**
- **2 whole star anise; or ¼ teaspoon crushed anise seeds and 2 cinnamon sticks (*each* 2 inches long)**
- **¾ teaspoon grated fresh ginger**
- **1 ounce dry thin pasta, such as capellini or coil vermicelli**

Cut peas diagonally into ¼- to ½-inch-wide slices. Set aside.

In a 4- to 5-quart pan, combine broth, star anise, and ginger. Bring to a boil over high heat. Add pasta; return to a boil and cook, uncovered, just until pasta is tender to bite (about 3 minutes; or time according to package directions). Add peas; return to a boil. Remove whole spices, then serve soup immediately. Makes 6 servings.

Per serving: 61 calories, 3 g protein, 8 g carbohydrates, 2 g total fat, 0 mg cholesterol, 1,036 mg sodium

■ ***To Microwave:*** Cut peas as directed. In a 4-quart microwave-safe casserole or tureen, combine broth, star anise, and ginger. Microwave, covered, on **HIGH (100%)** for 12 to 15 minutes or until mixture comes to a boil. Add pasta; microwave, covered, on **HIGH (100%)** for 4 to 6 minutes or until pasta is almost tender to bite, stirring once. Add peas; microwave, covered, on **HIGH (100%)** for 2 minutes. Let stand, covered, for 2 minutes.

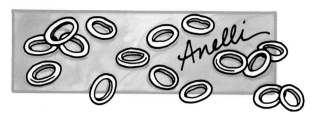

Winter Green Minestrone

Preparation time: About 30 minutes

Cooking time: About 2½ hours

Mustard greens and kale or cabbage add freshness to a classic supper. To preserve the greens' bright color and brisk flavor, stir the sliced leaves into the pot just minutes before serving.

- **3 quarts water**
- **3 pounds smoked ham hocks or shanks**
- **1 pound thin-skinned potatoes**
  Chicken bouillon cubes (optional)
- **½ cup dry elbow macaroni or anelli**
- **4 to 5 ounces mustard greens, rinsed well and drained**
- **5 to 6 ounces green or red kale or green, Savoy, or napa cabbage, rinsed well and drained**
- **1 package (10 oz.) or 2 cups frozen tiny peas**
  Salt and pepper
  Grated Parmesan cheese

In an 8- to 10-quart pan, combine water and ham hocks. Bring to a boil over high heat. Reduce heat, cover, and simmer until meat is tender when pierced (about 2 hours). Then lift out ham hocks and let stand until cool enough to handle. Pull meat from bones in bite-size shreds; discard skin, fat, and bones. Return meat to broth. (At this point, you may let cool, then cover and refrigerate for up to 2 days.)

Skim and discard fat from broth, then return broth to a boil over high heat. Meanwhile, scrub potatoes well; cut into ½-inch cubes. Taste broth; if desired, add bouillon cubes to enrich flavor. Add potatoes and macaroni to broth. Reduce heat, cover, and boil gently until potatoes are tender when pierced (10 to 15 minutes).

Meanwhile, cut mustard greens crosswise into ½-inch strips to make about 3 cups. Cut off and discard coarse stems from kale; cut leaves into shreds to make 1 quart. Add greens and peas to soup; then increase heat to medium-high and boil, uncovered, just until greens are wilted (2 to 3 minutes). Season to taste with salt and pepper. Serve with cheese to add to taste. Makes 6 to 8 servings.

Per serving: 208 calories, 13 g protein, 26 g carbohydrates, 6 g total fat, 28 mg cholesterol, 708 mg sodium

White Bean, Pasta & Sausage Soup

Pictured on facing page

Preparation time: 10 to 15 minutes

Cooking time: 2¼ to 2¾ hours

Thick with beans and shell-shaped pasta, this hearty soup makes a comforting supper dish. Serve with warm, crusty bread and a dessert of cheese and fresh fruit.

 1½ cups (about 8 oz.) dried Great Northern or small white beans
 8 ounces spicy Italian sausages
 1 large onion, chopped
 3 cloves garlic, minced or pressed
 1 large carrot (about 3 oz.), finely chopped
 2 tablespoons dried currants
 1 teaspoon dry basil
 1½ quarts regular-strength chicken broth
 3 cups water
 1 can (14½ oz.) pear-shaped tomatoes
 1 cup (about 3 oz.) dry large shell-shaped pasta
  Grated Parmesan cheese

Sort beans and discard any debris; rinse well and drain. Set beans aside.

Remove and discard casings from sausages, then crumble meat in large chunks into a 5- to 6-quart pan. Cook over high heat, stirring occasionally, until lightly browned (3 to 5 minutes). Discard all but 2 tablespoons of the fat. Add onion, garlic, and carrot; cook, stirring often, until onion begins to soften (2 to 3 minutes). Stir in beans, currants, basil, broth, and water. Bring to a boil; reduce heat, cover, and boil gently until beans are tender to bite (2 to 2½ hours).

Add tomatoes (break up with a spoon) and their liquid, then stir in pasta. Return to a boil; cover and boil gently until pasta is just tender to bite (about 12 minutes; or time according to package directions). Skim off and discard fat from soup. Serve soup with cheese to add to taste. Makes 4 to 6 servings.

Per serving: 448 calories, 23 g protein, 55 g carbohydrates, 16 g total fat, 30 mg cholesterol, 1,684 mg sodium

Pistou Soup with Sausage

Preparation time: About 35 minutes

Cooking time: About 1 hour and 20 minutes

This substantial whole-meal soup takes its name from *pistou*, a colorful Niçoise variation on pesto. You blend garlic, tomato paste, cheese, parsley, basil, and olive oil, then stir the pungent mixture into the soup as seasoning.

 1 pound leeks
 8 ounces linguisa sausages, cut into ½-inch-thick slices
 1 cup chopped carrots
 ½ cup dried split peas
 1½ cups diced thin-skinned potatoes
 1½ quarts *each* regular-strength chicken broth and water
  Pistou (recipe follows)
 8 ounces green beans, cut into 1-inch lengths
 3 ounces dry spaghetti, broken into 2-inch pieces

Cut off and discard all but 3 inches of green tops from leeks. Split leeks lengthwise and rinse well, then thinly slice crosswise. Set aside.

In a 6- to 8-quart pan, brown sausages over medium-high heat, stirring often. Discard all but 1 tablespoon of the fat. Add leeks and carrots; cook, stirring occasionally, until leeks are soft (about 8 minutes). Meanwhile, sort peas and discard any debris; rinse well and drain. To sausage-vegetable mixture, add peas, potatoes, broth, and water. Bring to a boil; reduce heat, cover, and boil gently until peas are soft to bite (about 1 hour). Meanwhile, prepare Pistou and set aside.

Add Pistou, beans, and spaghetti to soup. Increase heat to medium-high, bring to a boil, and boil until spaghetti is just tender to bite (6 to 8 minutes; or time according to package directions). Makes 8 servings.

Pistou. Combine 4 cloves **garlic** (minced or pressed), 1 can (6 oz.) **tomato paste**, ¾ cup grated **Parmesan cheese**, ¼ cup minced **parsley**, 1½ tablespoons **dry basil**, and ⅓ cup **olive oil**. Mix until well blended.

Per serving: 393 calories, 16 g protein, 35 g carbohydrates, 22 g total fat, 27 mg cholesterol, 1,285 mg sodium

*Plump pasta shells (conchiglie) mingle with vegetables
and spicy sausage in hearty White Bean, Pasta & Sausage
Soup (recipe on facing page). Balance the soup's richness
with a dessert of seasonal fresh fruit.*

Pinto Bean
& Pasta Soup

Preparation time: About 15 minutes

Cooking time: About 2½ hours

One of the most traditional of Italian soups is *pasta e fagioli*—pasta and beans cooked together in a thick, hearty broth. Smoky with bits of bacon, this version uses dried pinto beans or fresh red-and-white speckled cranberry beans.

    8   ounces (about 1¼ cups) dried pinto beans; or
        2½ cups fresh-shelled cranberry beans (2½ lbs.
        unshelled)
    1   pound sliced bacon, cut into 1-inch pieces
    1   large onion, coarsely chopped
    3   stalks celery, cut into ½-inch-thick slices
    6   cloves garlic, minced or pressed
    2   teaspoons dry oregano leaves
    2   quarts water
    1   can (14½ oz. to 1 lb.) tomatoes
    2   ounces dry fettuccine, broken into 2-inch
        pieces
        Salt and pepper
        Freshly grated Parmesan cheese

If using dried beans, sort beans and discard any debris; rinse well and drain. Set beans aside.

In a 5- to 6-quart pan, cook bacon over medium-low heat until crisp, stirring often. Lift out, drain, crumble, and set aside. Discard all but ¼ cup of the drippings.

To reserved drippings, add onion, celery, garlic, and oregano. Cook, stirring, for 5 minutes. Add dried or fresh-shelled beans and water. Increase heat to high and bring to a boil; reduce heat, cover, and boil gently until beans are tender to bite (about 2 hours for dried beans, 45 minutes to 1 hour for fresh-shelled beans).

Add tomatoes (break up with a spoon) and their liquid. Stir in fettuccine, cover, and boil gently, stirring occasionally, just until tender to bite (8 to 10 minutes; or time according to package directions). Season to taste with salt and pepper. Serve with bacon and cheese to add to taste. Makes 6 to 8 servings.

Per serving: 328 calories, 14 g protein, 33 g carbohydrates, 16 g total fat, 28 mg cholesterol, 452 mg sodium

Red Bean
& Lamb Soup

Preparation time: About 20 minutes

Cooking time: About 3½ hours

Rice-shaped pasta or *orzo* (similar shapes are called *riso* and *seme di melone*) lends substance to this full-meal soup. You'll detect Greek influences in the flavors of mint, rosemary, cinnamon, and lemon—and in the garnish of crumbled feta cheese.

    8   ounces (about 1¼ cups) dried red kidney
        beans, pinto beans, or pink beans
    ¼   cup salad oil
    4   lamb shanks (about 4 lbs. *total*), cracked
    2   medium-size onions, chopped
    ½   cup finely chopped fresh mint or
        2 tablespoons dry mint
    ½   teaspoon *each* dry rosemary and ground
        cinnamon
    2   quarts water
    ⅓   cup (about 2 oz.) dry rice-shaped pasta
    2   tablespoons tomato paste
    4   cloves garlic, minced or pressed
    3   tablespoons lemon juice
        Salt and pepper
    4   ounces feta cheese, crumbled into ½-inch
        pieces
        Lemon wedges

Sort beans and discard any debris; rinse well and drain. Set beans aside.

Heat 2 tablespoons of the oil in a 6- to 8-quart pan over medium heat. Add lamb shanks and brown evenly on all sides (about 20 minutes). Lift lamb from pan; add remaining 2 tablespoons oil, onions, mint, rosemary, and cinnamon. Cook for 5 minutes, stirring often.

Return lamb to pan; add beans and water. Bring to a boil. Reduce heat, cover, and boil gently until meat is very tender and pulls easily from bones (about 3 hours).

Skim and discard fat from soup, then stir in pasta, tomato paste, garlic, and lemon juice. Cover and continue to cook until pasta is tender to bite (about 10 minutes; or time according to package directions). Season to taste with salt and pepper. Serve with cheese and lemon wedges to season soup to taste. Makes 6 to 8 servings.

Per serving: 490 calories, 48 g protein, 30 g carbohydrates, 19 g total fat, 129 mg cholesterol, 337 mg sodium

Mediterranean Pasta Soup

Preparation time: About 20 minutes

Cooking time: About 2½ hours

It all adds up to mealtime satisfaction in wintery weather: *tripolini* (tiny ruffled bow ties) combined with small white beans, vegetables, and just enough crumbled Italian sausage to lend a mildly spicy flavor. Sprinkle chopped tomato and shredded Swiss cheese atop each serving to taste.

½ cup (about 3½ oz.) dried small white beans
4 ounces mild Italian sausages
1 small onion, finely chopped
2 cloves garlic, minced or pressed
1½ teaspoons dry thyme leaves
¼ teaspoon pepper
3 quarts regular-strength chicken broth
1 teaspoon grated lemon peel
2 small carrots (about 3 oz. *total*), cut lengthwise into quarters, then thinly sliced crosswise
2 stalks celery, finely chopped
1 cup (about 4½ oz.) dry tripolini or small shell-shaped pasta
1 small tomato (about 4 oz.), cut into ½-inch cubes (optional)
1 cup (4 oz.) shredded Swiss cheese (optional)

Sort beans and discard any debris; rinse well and drain. Set beans aside.

Remove and discard casings from sausages, then crumble meat into a 4- to 5-quart pan. Cook over medium heat, stirring often, until lightly browned (about 4 minutes). Add onion, garlic, thyme, and pepper; cook, stirring occasionally, until onion begins to brown (about 5 minutes). Add beans, broth, and lemon peel. Increase heat to high and bring to a boil. Reduce heat, cover, and boil gently until beans are tender to bite (about 2 hours).

Add carrots, celery, and pasta. Increase heat to high and bring to a boil. Cover, reduce heat, and boil gently until carrots and pasta are just tender to bite (8 to 10 minutes; or time according to package directions).

Ladle soup into bowls. Offer tomato and cheese, if desired, to sprinkle over soup to taste. Makes 6 to 8 servings.

Per serving: 243 calories, 12 g protein, 30 g carbohydrates, 9 g total fat, 12 mg cholesterol, 1,859 mg sodium

Hoppin' John Soup

Preparation time: About 30 minutes

Cooking time: About 3 hours and 20 minutes

Named for a traditional Southern dish, this soup features black-eyed peas and greens along with tiny soup pasta such as stars (*stelline* or *stellette*) or circles (*occhi di pernice*—"partridge eyes").

8 ounces (about 1¼ cups) dried black-eyed peas or baby lima beans
3 tablespoons salad oil
1 pound *each* turnips and carrots, diced
1 medium-size red bell pepper (about 5 oz.), seeded and chopped
½ to 1 teaspoon crushed dried hot red chiles
About 2 pounds smoked ham hocks or shanks
2 quarts water
⅓ cup (about 2 oz.) dry tiny star- or circle-shaped pasta
8 ounces mustard greens, rinsed well and drained

Sort peas and discard any debris; rinse well and drain. Set peas aside.

Heat oil in a 6- to 8-quart pan over medium heat. Add turnips, carrots, bell pepper, and chiles; cook for 5 minutes, stirring often. Add ham hocks, peas, and water. Increase heat to high and bring to a boil. Reduce heat, cover, and boil gently until meat is very tender and pulls easily from bones (about 3 hours).

Skim and discard fat from soup, then stir in pasta. Cover and cook until pasta is tender to bite (about 10 minutes; or time according to package directions). Meanwhile, chop greens; stir into soup just before serving. Makes 6 to 8 servings.

Per serving: 307 calories, 17 g protein, 39 g carbohydrates, 10 g total fat, 18 mg cholesterol, 507 mg sodium

Sizzling and smoky from the barbecue, hot chicken is a delicious foil for cool vegetables and gemelli (pasta twists). Serve Grilled Chicken & Pasta Primavera (recipe on facing page) on a spring evening, accompanied with warm corn sticks and iced tea.

18

Salads

*V*ersatile and adaptable, salads based on pasta range from elegant first courses such as Stir-fried Asparagus & Scallops on Cool Pasta to casual potluck contributions like Antipasto Pasta Salad. You can serve them at room temperature or cold, and some—Hot Pasta & Tuna Salad, for example—are even brought forth steaming hot.

Virtually any size or shape of pasta can slip temptingly into a salad; choices in this chapter include plump tortellini, svelte vermicelli, and engaging little corkscrews. We've even concocted a memorable salad with won ton wrappers—they're cut into strips, baked until crisp, and topped with fresh spinach and chicken in a sesame dressing.

Pictured on facing page

Grilled Chicken & Pasta Primavera Salad

Preparation time: About 25 minutes

Cooking time: About 30 minutes

You'll enjoy the tantalizing hot and cold contrasts of this colorful salad, a good choice for a warm-weather main dish.

> Balsamic Dressing (page 20)
> 8 ounces dry gemelli or other bite-size pasta twists or spirals
> ½ cup frozen peas, thawed
> ¼ cup thinly sliced green onions (including tops)
> 2 whole chicken breasts (about 1 lb. *each*), skinned, boned, and split
> 2 medium-size carrots (about 4 oz. *total*), thinly sliced
> 12 ounces asparagus, tough ends snapped off, spears cut into ½-inch-long pieces (keep stems and tips separate)
> 4 ounces mushrooms, thinly sliced
> Red oak leaf lettuce leaves or small inner red leaf lettuce leaves, washed and crisped
> Slivered green onions (including tops)

Prepare Balsamic Dressing and set aside.

In a 5- to 6-quart pan, cook pasta in 3 quarts boiling water just until tender to bite (8 to 10 minutes); or cook according to package directions. Drain, rinse with cold water, and drain well again. Place pasta in a large bowl and lightly mix in peas, sliced onions, and ½ cup of the dressing. Set aside.

Rinse chicken and pat dry, then brush on all sides with some of the remaining dressing. Place on a greased grill 4 to 6 inches above a solid bed of medium-hot coals. Cook, brushing with remaining dressing and turning once, until meat in thickest part is no longer pink; cut to test (18 to 20 minutes *total*).

Meanwhile, in a medium-size pan, bring 2 cups of water to a boil over high heat. Add carrots. Return water to a boil, then add asparagus stems; return to a boil again and add asparagus tips. Return water to a boil a third time and boil vegetables for 1 minute; then drain, rinse with cold water, and drain well again. Lightly mix blanched vegetables and mushrooms into pasta mixture.

Line 4 dinner plates with lettuce. Divide pasta mixture among plates; garnish with slivered onions. Slice each chicken breast half crosswise into ½-inch-wide strips, cutting on a slight diagonal. Arrange hot chicken attractively to one side of pasta salad on each plate; serve at once. Makes 4 servings.

Balsamic Dressing. Combine 3 tablespoons **balsamic vinegar,** 1 large clove **garlic** (minced or pressed), ½ teaspoon **crushed dried hot red chiles,** 2 tablespoons grated **Parmesan cheese,** and ½ cup **olive oil.** Mix until well blended; season to taste with **salt,** if desired, and freshly ground **pepper.**

Per serving: 670 calories, 46 g protein, 52 g carbohydrates, 31 g total fat, 88 mg cholesterol, 176 mg sodium

Crisp Won Ton Salad

Preparation time: About 35 minutes

Baking time: About 6 minutes

Cooking time: About 20 minutes

Ready-made won ton wrappers—sliced, buttered, and baked—make a crisp bed for this hot main-dish salad of stir-fried vegetables and chicken with fresh spinach.

Gemelli

Crisp Won Ton Strips (recipe follows)
Sesame-Lemon Dressing (recipe on facing page)

- 12 ounces spinach, rinsed well
- 5 teaspoons salad oil
- 1 small onion, thinly sliced
- ½ cup thinly sliced celery
- 1 large carrot (about 3 oz.), cut into 1-inch-long matchstick pieces
- 1 tablespoon finely chopped fresh ginger
- 2 tablespoons water
- 1 whole chicken breast (about 1 lb.), skinned, boned, and cut into ¼-inch-thick bite-size strips
- 1 can (about 5 oz.) sliced water chestnuts, drained
- ½ cup salted roasted peanuts
- ½ cup thinly sliced green onions (including tops)

Prepare Crisp Won Ton Strips and Sesame-Lemon Dressing; set aside. Pat spinach dry. Remove and discard stems; cover and refrigerate leaves while preparing salad.

Place a wide frying pan or wok over medium heat. When pan is hot, add 2 teaspoons of the oil, then the sliced small onion; cook, stirring occasionally, until onion is pale golden (2 to 3 minutes). Add celery, carrot, ginger, and water; cover and cook, stirring occasionally, until carrot is tender-crisp to bite (3 to 4 minutes). Transfer the vegetable mixture to a bowl and set aside.

Add 2 teaspoons more oil to pan and increase heat to high. Add half the chicken strips. Cook until browned on bottom, then stir-fry until meat is opaque throughout; cut to test (about 3 minutes). Add chicken to vegetables. Heat remaining 1 teaspoon oil in pan; add remaining chicken and cook as just directed. Then pour chicken-vegetable mixture from bowl back into pan; add water chestnuts, peanuts, and 3 tablespoons of the dressing. Stir-fry until hot (about 3 minutes).

Divide spinach among 4 or 5 dinner plates; top with Crisp Won Ton Strips. Spoon hot chicken mixture over won tons; sprinkle with green onions. Offer remaining dressing to add to salad to taste. Makes 5 servings.

Crisp Won Ton Strips. Cut 1 package (7 oz.; or use half of a 14-oz. package) **won ton wrappers** into ½-inch-wide strips. Melt about 1 tablespoon **butter** or margarine. Brush a baking sheet lightly with some of the melted butter; arrange won ton strips close together in a single layer on baking sheet, then brush lightly with a little more butter.

Bake, uncovered, in a 375° oven until light golden (about 6 minutes). Pour onto a rack to cool. Repeat to bake remaining strips. If made ahead, package cooled strips airtight and store at room temperature for up to 2 days.

Per serving of salad (without dressing): 373 calories, 24 g protein, 38 g carbohydrates, 15 g total fat, 40 mg cholesterol, 263 mg sodium

Sesame-Lemon Dressing. Combine ½ cup **seasoned rice vinegar** (or ½ cup rice vinegar or white wine vinegar mixed with 1½ teaspoons sugar); 2 tablespoons *each* **soy sauce** and **Oriental sesame oil;** 1 tablespoon **lemon juice;** and ⅛ teaspoon **chili oil** or ground red pepper (cayenne). Mix until well blended. Makes about ¾ cup.

Per tablespoon of dressing: 25 calories, 0.2 g protein, 1 g carbohydrates, 2 g total fat, 0 mg cholesterol, 172 mg sodium

Hot Pasta & Tuna Salad

Preparation time: About 15 minutes

Cooking time: About 15 minutes

Ripe olives, roasted peppers, and a chile-caper dressing brighten this hot main-dish salad. Use oil- or water-packed tuna, as you prefer.

> **Chile Dressing (recipe follows)**
> 12 ounces dry large shell-shaped pasta
> 1 tablespoon olive oil
> 1 jar (7 oz.) roasted red peppers, drained and cut into thin strips
> ⅓ cup finely chopped parsley
> 1 can (3½ oz.) pitted ripe olives, drained
> 1 large can (12½ oz.) chunk-style tuna, drained
> Salt and freshly ground pepper

Prepare Chile Dressing and set aside.

In a 5- to 6-quart pan, cook pasta in 3 quarts boiling water just until tender to bite (about 12 minutes); or cook according to package directions. Drain well and set aside.

While pasta is cooking, heat oil in a wide frying pan over medium-high heat. Add roasted peppers, parsley, olives, and tuna. Stir gently until hot (about 2 minutes). Mix in half the dressing.

In a large bowl, lightly mix pasta and remaining dressing. Add tuna mixture; lift with 2 spoons to mix gently. Season to taste with salt and pepper. Makes 6 servings.

Chile Dressing. Combine ⅓ cup **olive oil,** 3 tablespoons **wine vinegar,** 2 tablespoons drained **capers,** ½ teaspoon **crushed dried hot red chiles,** and 2 cloves **garlic** (minced or pressed). Mix well.

Per serving: 446 calories, 23 g protein, 46 g carbohydrates, 19 g total fat, 22 mg cholesterol, 397 mg sodium

Vermicelli

Stir-fried Asparagus & Scallops on Cool Pasta

Preparation time: 10 minutes

Cooking time: 10 to 15 minutes

For an elegant first course, top thin pasta strands with a refreshing combination of scallops and sliced asparagus in a light rice vinegar dressing.

> 8 ounces dry capellini or coil vermicelli
> 8 ounces bay scallops or sea scallops, rinsed and drained
> 3 tablespoons salad oil
> 1 pound asparagus, tough ends snapped off, spears cut diagonally into ¼-inch-thick, 1½- to 2-inch-long slices
> 3 tablespoons water
> 1 clove garlic, minced or pressed
> 1 tablespoon minced fresh ginger
> ½ cup rice vinegar; or ½ cup white wine vinegar mixed with 1 teaspoon sugar
> 2 tablespoons sugar
> 1 teaspoon *each* soy sauce and Oriental sesame oil

In a 5- to 6-quart pan, cook capellini in 3 quarts boiling water just until barely tender to bite (about 3 minutes); or cook according to package directions. Drain, rinse with cold water, and drain well again. Place in a shallow dish. If using sea scallops, cut scallops into ½-inch pieces. Set aside.

Place a wok or wide frying pan over high heat. Add 1 tablespoon of the salad oil, then asparagus; stir to coat with oil. Add 3 tablespoons water; cover and cook just until asparagus is tender-crisp to bite (2 to 3 minutes). Lift out asparagus and spoon over pasta.

Add remaining 2 tablespoons salad oil, garlic, ginger, and scallops to pan. Cook, stirring, until scallops are opaque throughout; cut to test (2 to 3 minutes). Add vinegar, sugar, soy, and sesame oil; cook, stirring, just until sugar is dissolved. Pour over pasta mixture. If made ahead, cover and refrigerate for up to 4 hours. Makes 4 to 6 servings.

Per serving: 326 calories, 15 g protein, 44 g carbohydrates, 10 g total fat, 15 mg cholesterol, 144 mg sodium

Pictured on facing page

Tortellini, Shrimp & Pesto Salad

Preparation time: About 15 minutes

Cooking time: 5 to 20 minutes

Chilling time: At least 1 hour

Here's a salad that's perfect for picnics and potlucks. You can make it the night before, then refrigerate it to let the flavors blend. Both fresh and dry tortellini work well in this recipe.

Pesto Dressing (recipe follows)
1 package (9 oz.) fresh tortellini or 1 package (7 or 8 oz.) dry tortellini
1 medium-size red bell pepper (about 5 oz.), seeded and cut into thin bite-size strips
6 ounces tiny cooked and shelled shrimp

Prepare Pesto Dressing and set aside.

In a 4- to 5-quart pan, cook tortellini in 3 quarts boiling water just until tender to bite (4 to 6 minutes for fresh tortellini, 15 to 20 minutes for dry); or cook according to package directions. Drain, rinse with cold water, and drain well again.

In a large bowl, lightly mix the tortellini, Pesto Dressing, bell pepper strips, and shrimp. Cover mixture and refrigerate for at least 1 hour or up to 8 hours. Makes 4 servings.

Pesto Dressing. In a blender or food processor, combine 1 cup lightly packed **fresh basil leaves** (or ¾ cup fresh parsley leaves and 2 tablespoons dry basil); 1 large clove **garlic**, coarsely chopped; ½ cup grated **Parmesan cheese**; 2½ tablespoons **red wine vinegar**; and ½ cup **olive oil**. Whirl until puréed.

Per serving: 538 calories, 24 g protein, 35 g carbohydrates, 34 g total fat, 126 mg cholesterol, 569 mg sodium

Antipasto Pasta Salad

Preparation time: About 30 minutes

Cooking time: About 40 minutes

The brightly colored ingredients of an Italian appetizer—fresh vegetables, shiny black olives, prosciutto, and Parmesan cheese—join pasta spirals in a raspberry vinaigrette.

Cooked Artichoke Hearts (recipe follows) or 1 can (8½ oz.) artichoke hearts packed in water, drained
10 ounces dry bite-size pasta twists or spirals such as rotelle or fusilli
Raspberry Vinaigrette (recipe follows)
3 cups broccoli flowerets
1 cup pitted ripe olives
4 ounces mushrooms, thinly sliced
1 cup quartered cherry tomatoes
2 ounces prosciutto or cooked ham, cut into thin bite-size strips
1 cup (about 5 oz.) finely shredded Asiago or Parmesan cheese

If using fresh artichokes, prepare Cooked Artichoke Hearts and set aside.

In a 5- to 6-quart pan, cook pasta in 3 quarts boiling water just until tender to bite (12 to 15 minutes); or cook according to package directions. Drain, rinse with cold water, and drain well again. While pasta is cooking, prepare Raspberry Vinaigrette and set aside.

Steam broccoli, covered, on a rack over 1 inch of boiling water until barely tender when pierced (about 5 minutes). Rinse with cold water and drain well.

In a large bowl, combine pasta, broccoli, artichokes, olives, mushrooms, tomatoes, prosciutto, cheese, and Raspberry Vinaigrette; mix lightly. If made ahead, cover and refrigerate for up to 8 hours. Makes 8 to 10 servings.

Cooked Artichoke Hearts. Break tough outer leaves from 10 small **artichokes** (*each* about 2 inches in diameter), leaving only the pale, edible inner leaves. Trim and discard thorny tips of leaves; peel bases of artichokes. In a large pan, cook artichokes, uncovered, in 2 quarts **boiling water** until tender when pierced (about 20 minutes). Drain well; when cool enough to handle, cut into quarters.

Raspberry Vinaigrette. Combine ½ cup **raspberry vinegar**, ⅔ cup **olive oil**, 1½ teaspoons **dry basil**, and ¼ teaspoon **pepper**. Mix until well blended.

Per serving: 391 calories, 14 g protein, 31 g carbohydrates, 24 g total fat, 14 mg cholesterol, 484 mg sodium

Make the most of summer's abundance of fragrant fresh basil—whirl it into an aromatic dressing for easy Tortellini, Shrimp & Pesto Salad (recipe on facing page). Tote the salad along to your next picnic; it's great for dining al fresco.

23

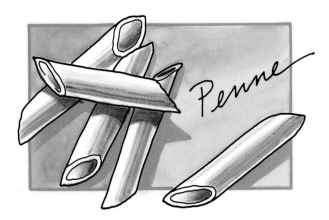

Penne

Penne with Tomato & Basil Mignonette

Preparation time: About 10 minutes

Cooking time: 15 to 20 minutes.

Standing time: About 15 minutes

The sweet summer flavor of vine-ripened tomatoes permeates *al dente* pasta in this lean and refreshing red, white, and green salad.

    2 tablespoons pine nuts
       Basil Mignonette Dressing (recipe follows)
    8 ounces dry penne or other small tube-shaped
       pasta, such as pennette or mostaccioli
    2 large tomatoes (about 12 oz. *total*), seeded and
       chopped
       Salt (optional)
       Fresh basil sprigs

Stir pine nuts in a small frying pan over medium-low heat until lightly browned (about 3 minutes). Set nuts aside. Prepare Basil Mignonette Dressing and set aside.

In a 5- to 6-quart pan, cook pasta in 3 quarts boiling water just until tender to bite (10 to 12 minutes); or cook according to package directions. Drain, rinse with cold water, and drain well again.

In a large bowl, lightly mix pasta, dressing, and tomatoes; season to taste with salt, if desired. Let stand at room temperature for about 15 minutes. Mix lightly; sprinkle with pine nuts and garnish with basil sprigs, then serve. Makes 4 to 6 servings.

Basil Mignonette Dressing. Combine ¼ cup **dry white wine;** 2 tablespoons *each* **lemon juice,** finely chopped **shallot,** and slivered **fresh basil leaves;** and ¼ teaspoon freshly ground **pepper.** Mix until well blended.

Per serving: 211 calories, 7 g protein, 39 g carbohydrates, 3 g total fat, 0 mg cholesterol, 9 mg sodium

Sesame Noodle Salad

Preparation time: About 30 minutes

Cooking time: About 15 minutes

Chilling time: At least 2 hours

Thin noodles flecked with sesame seeds and stir-fried vegetables make a good picnic accompaniment to cold roast chicken.

       Sesame Seed Dressing (recipe on facing page)
    8 medium-size fresh or dried shiitake mush-
       rooms or large fresh regular mushrooms
    8 ounces dry vermicelli (not coil vermicelli)
    3 tablespoons salad oil
    2 teaspoons minced fresh ginger
    4 ounces green beans, cut diagonally into
       ¼-inch-thick slices
    2 medium-size carrots (about 4 oz. *total*), cut
       into 1-inch-long matchstick pieces
    2 medium-size crookneck squash (about 8 oz.
       total), cut into 1-inch-long matchstick pieces
    1 tablespoon *each* soy sauce and dry sherry
       Salt
    2 or 3 green onions, ends trimmed

Prepare Sesame Seed Dressing and set aside.

If using dried mushrooms, soak in warm water to cover until soft and pliable (20 to 30 minutes). Cut off and discard stems; set caps aside. If using fresh mushrooms, set caps aside and cut stems into thin strips.

Meanwhile, in a 5- to 6-quart pan, cook vermicelli in 3 quarts boiling water just until tender to bite (8 to 10 minutes); or cook according to package directions. Drain, rinse with cold water, and drain well again. Transfer to a large bowl and set aside.

Heat 2 tablespoons of the oil in a wide frying pan over high heat. Add ginger, beans, carrots, squash, and slivered fresh mushroom stems. Stir-fry just until vegetables are barely tender-crisp to bite (1 to 1½ minutes). Lift vegetables from pan and add to vermicelli.

Reduce heat to medium. Add remaining 1 tablespoon oil, soy, sherry, and mushroom caps to pan. Cover pan if using dried mushrooms; leave uncovered if using fresh mushrooms. Cook, turning occasionally, until mushrooms have absorbed all liquid (about 2 minutes). Set aside.

Add Sesame Seed Dressing to vermicelli mixture, then mix lightly. Season to taste with salt. Cover and refrigerate, stirring occasionally, for at least 2 hours or until next day. Garnish with mushroom caps and whole green onions. Makes 4 to 6 servings.

Sesame Seed Dressing. Heat ¼ cup **salad oil** in a wide frying pan over medium-low heat. Add 3 tablespoons **sesame seeds** and cook, uncovered, until golden (about 2 minutes). Remove from heat and let cool slightly.

Combine ⅓ cup **sugar,** ½ cup **distilled white vinegar,** and 2 tablespoons **dry sherry;** stir until sugar is dissolved. Blend sesame-oil mixture into sugar mixture.

Per serving: 288 calories, 8 g protein, 45 g carbohydrates, 9 g total fat, 0 mg cholesterol, 218 mg sodium

Broccoli, Pasta & Bean Salad

Preparation time: About 10 minutes

Cooking time: About 15 minutes

A mustard-seasoned olive oil and red wine vinegar dressing brings together the flavors of pasta and vegetables in this simple salad.

- 1 **pound broccoli**
- 2 **cups (about 6 oz.) dry large shell-shaped pasta**
- ½ **cup olive oil**
- ¼ **cup red wine vinegar**
- 1 **tablespoon Dijon mustard**
- ½ **teaspoon dry basil**
- 1 **can (about 15 oz.) red kidney beans, drained and rinsed**
  Salt and pepper

Trim and discard tough ends from broccoli stalks. Thinly slice tender portion of stalks crosswise; cut tops into bite-size flowerets. Set all broccoli aside.

In a 5- to 6-quart pan, cook pasta in 3 quarts boiling water just until barely tender to bite (10 to 12 minutes); or cook according to package directions. Drop broccoli into boiling water and cook just until it turns bright green (1 to 2 minutes). Drain pasta and broccoli, rinse with cold water, and drain well again.

While pasta and broccoli are cooking, combine oil, vinegar, mustard, and basil in a large bowl. Mix until well blended, then add drained pasta, broccoli, and beans; mix gently. Season to taste with salt and pepper. If made ahead, cover and refrigerate for up to 2 hours. Makes 6 to 8 servings.

Per serving: 279 calories, 7 g protein, 28 g carbohydrates, 16 g total fat, 0 mg cholesterol, 300 mg sodium

Summertime Pasta Salad

Preparation time: About 25 minutes

Chilling time: At least 2 hours

Cooking time: 12 to 15 minutes

This salad is so flavorful you won't notice that it's made without oil. Pasta twists and an abundance of summer vegetables are accented with savory herbs and grated Parmesan cheese.

- 3 **small tomatoes (about 12 oz.** *total***), peeled and chopped**
- 1 **cup** *each* **thinly sliced green onions (including tops), finely chopped celery, finely chopped green bell pepper, and diced zucchini**
- 2 **cloves garlic, minced or pressed**
- 3 **tablespoons white wine vinegar**
- 1 **tablespoon sugar**
- ⅓ **cup chopped fresh basil**
- 1 **teaspoon chopped fresh rosemary**
- ½ **to 1 teaspoon chopped fresh oregano**
  Salt and coarsely ground pepper
- 8 **ounces dry bite-size pasta twists or spirals such as rotelle or fusilli**
- ⅓ **to ⅔ cup grated Parmesan cheese**

In a large bowl, combine tomatoes, onions, celery, bell pepper, zucchini, garlic, vinegar, sugar, basil, and rosemary. Mix lightly, then season to taste with oregano, salt, and pepper; mix well. Cover and refrigerate for at least 2 hours or for up to 8 hours.

Shortly before serving, in a 5- to 6-quart pan, cook pasta in 3 quarts boiling water just until tender to bite (12 to 15 minutes); or cook according to package directions. Drain, rinse with cold water, and drain well again. Pour into a serving bowl or rimmed platter.

To serve, spoon tomato mixture over pasta; mix lightly with 2 forks, then sprinkle with 2 tablespoons of the cheese. Serve with remaining cheese to add to taste. Makes 8 servings.

Per serving: 161 calories, 7 g protein, 28 g carbohydrates, 2 g total fat, 5 mg cholesterol, 132 mg sodium

A quartet of flavorful vegetables tops fresh green pasta in
Parsley Pesto Grilled Vegetables & Spinach Fettuccine
(recipe on facing page). The pungent pesto doubles as a
baste for the vegetables and a sauce for the noodles.

Vegetables & Cheese

Liberal quantities of bright vegetables and sharp or mellow cheeses are favorite additions to pasta of all sorts, in dishes that can enliven your menus throughout the year. Fascinating first courses, substantial main dishes, winning side dishes—you'll find them all among the appealing choices in this chapter. Pasta and vegetable lovers will applaud our updated lasagne (it's meatless), plump tortellini in a creamy sauce thick with mushrooms, and a fresh new version of popular pasta primavera.

For some novel ways with pesto, see page 33; we show you how to make the famous sauce with a variety of herbs and greens. And for a taste of trompe l'oeil, *have a look at the ingenious ways vegetables can masquerade as pasta (page 44).*

Pictured on facing page

Parsley Pesto Grilled Vegetables & Spinach Fettuccine

Preparation time: About 10 minutes

Cooking time: About 15 minutes

For a colorful vegetarian meal from the barbecue, arrange savory grilled vegetables over a mound of tender green fettuccine. If you'd like to add meat, serve juicy Italian sausages as an accompaniment; put them on the grill before you add the first vegetables.

Parsley Pesto (page 28)
4 small zucchini (10 to 12 oz. *total*)
2 small Japanese eggplants (about 8 oz. *total*), halved lengthwise
4 small pear-shaped (Roma-type) tomatoes (about 6 oz. *total*), halved lengthwise
1 medium-size red onion, unpeeled, quartered
1 package (9 oz.) fresh green fettuccine
½ cup whipping cream
⅓ to ½ cup grated Parmesan cheese

Prepare Parsley Pesto; set aside.

Cutting toward stem end, slice each zucchini lengthwise into thin strips, leaving strips attached at stem so they can be fanned out. Brush cut surfaces of zucchini, eggplants, tomatoes, and onion with some of the pesto.

Place vegetables, cut sides down, on a greased grill 4 to 6 inches above a bed of medium-hot coals. Cook until vegetables are just tender when pierced (about 3 minutes for tomatoes, 4 to 5 minutes for zucchini, and 8 to 10 minutes for eggplant and onion). As each vegetable is cooked, remove it from grill and keep warm.

In a 5- to 6-quart pan, cook fettuccine in 3 quarts boiling water just until tender to bite (3 to 4 minutes); or cook according to package directions. Drain well.

In a wide frying pan, combine cream and remaining Parsley Pesto; bring to a boil over high heat. Remove from heat; quickly add pasta and mix lightly, using 2 spoons. Divide among 4 dinner plates. Arrange vegetables over pasta, spreading zucchini into fans. Serve with cheese to add to taste. Makes 4 servings.

Parsley Pesto. In a food processor or blender, combine 1½ cups lightly packed **Italian (flat-leaf) parsley**, ¾ cup grated **Parmesan cheese**, ⅔ cup **olive oil**, and 3 cloves **garlic**, coarsely chopped; whirl until smoothly puréed. Season to taste with **salt** and freshly ground **pepper**.

Per serving: 756 calories, 22 g protein, 47 g carbohydrates, 55 g total fat, 124 mg cholesterol, 517 mg sodium

Vermicelli with Vegetable Sauce

Preparation time: 15 to 20 minutes

Cooking time: About 50 minutes

This slowly simmered, vegetable-rich red sauce is so filled with savory flavor that you'll never even miss the meat.

- 2 tablespoons olive oil or salad oil
- 1 medium-size onion, finely chopped
- 1 teaspoon *each* dry basil, dry tarragon, fennel seeds, and dry oregano leaves
- 1 clove garlic, minced or pressed
- 1 small zucchini (about 3 oz.), thinly sliced
- 4 ounces mushrooms, thinly sliced
- 1 small green bell pepper (about 4 oz.), seeded and finely chopped
- ½ cup dry red wine
- 1 pound (about 3 medium-size) tomatoes, peeled, seeded, and chopped
- 1 can (6 oz.) tomato paste
- 1 teaspoon sugar
  Salt and pepper
- 10 to 12 ounces dry vermicelli (not coil vermicelli) or spaghettini
- ½ to ¾ cup grated Parmesan cheese

Heat oil in a 3- to 3½-quart pan over medium heat. Add onion, basil, tarragon, fennel seeds, and oregano; cook, stirring often, until onion begins to soften (about 5 minutes). Stir in garlic, zucchini, mushrooms, and bell pepper. Cook, stirring often, until mushrooms begin to brown (8 to 10 minutes).

Add wine, tomatoes, tomato paste, and sugar. Increase heat to high and bring mixture to a boil; reduce heat, cover, and simmer until sauce is thick (about 35 minutes), stirring occasionally. Season to taste with salt and pepper.

When sauce is almost done, in a 5- to 6-quart pan, cook vermicelli in 3 quarts boiling water just until tender to bite (8 to 10 minutes); or cook according to package directions. Drain pasta well, then divide among 6 dinner plates and top with sauce. Serve with cheese to add to taste. Makes 6 servings.

Per serving: 330 calories, 13 g protein, 53 g carbohydrates, 8 g total fat, 7 mg cholesterol, 390 mg sodium

Seashells with Cauliflower Sauce

Preparation time: About 12 minutes

Cooking time: About 25 minutes

For a hearty winter main dish, stir cauliflower and little pasta seashells into a bright tomato-wine sauce; pass Parmesan cheese to sprinkle on top.

- ¼ cup olive oil
- ½ teaspoon dry thyme leaves
- 1 medium-size onion, thinly sliced
- 1 medium-size carrot (about 2 oz.), coarsely shredded
- 2 cloves garlic, minced or pressed
- 1 large can (28 oz.) pear-shaped tomatoes
- ½ cup dry white wine
- 8 ounces dry small shell-shaped pasta
- 2 cups coarsely chopped cauliflower
  Salt and freshly ground pepper
  Chopped parsley
- ⅓ to ½ cup grated Parmesan cheese

Heat oil in a wide frying pan over medium heat. Add thyme, onion, and carrot; cook, uncovered, stirring often, until onion is soft but not brown (about 5 minutes). Stir in garlic, tomatoes (break up with a spoon) and their liquid, and wine. Bring to a boil; reduce heat, cover, and boil gently for 10 minutes. Then uncover, increase heat to medium-high, and cook, stirring occasionally, until sauce is thick (about 10 minutes).

Meanwhile, in a 5- to 6-quart pan, cook pasta in 3 quarts boiling water just until tender to bite (10 to 12 minutes); or cook according to package directions. Drain well. While pasta is cooking, steam cauliflower, covered, on a rack over 1 inch of boiling water until barely tender when pierced (about 5 minutes); remove from heat and set aside.

Season sauce to taste with salt and pepper. Add pasta and cauliflower to sauce; mix lightly. Sprinkle with parsley. Serve with cheese to add to taste. Makes 4 servings.

Per serving: 440 calories, 14 g protein, 59 g carbohydrates, 17 g total fat, 7 mg cholesterol, 496 mg sodium

Straw & Hay in Tomato Cream

Preparation time: About 15 minutes

Cooking time: About 20 minutes

Known as *paglia e fieno* in Italian, this colorful dish combines thinly cut yellow and green pasta. Look for the pasta in your supermarket, in either the dry pasta section or the refrigerator case.

 1 tablespoon olive oil
 5 medium-size pear-shaped (Roma-type) tomatoes (10 to 12 oz. *total*), seeded and chopped
 1 clove garlic, minced or pressed
 2 tablespoons chopped fresh basil or 1 teaspoon dry basil
 ¼ teaspoon salt
 ⅛ teaspoon ground white pepper
 ½ cup dry white wine
 8 ounces dry yellow and green tagliarini or 4½ ounces (half of a 9-oz. package) *each* fresh yellow and green linguine
 1 cup whipping cream
 1 tablespoon lemon juice
  Fresh basil sprigs
 ⅓ to ½ cup grated Parmesan cheese

Heat oil in a wide frying pan over medium heat; add tomatoes, garlic, chopped basil, salt, white pepper, and wine. Bring to a boil over medium-high heat. Cook, uncovered, stirring often, until tomatoes are soft and almost all liquid has evaporated (8 to 10 minutes). Transfer mixture to a food processor or blender and whirl until puréed; return to pan.

In a 5- to 6-quart pan, cook pasta in 3 quarts boiling water just until tender to bite (6 to 7 minutes for dry pasta, 1 to 2 minutes for fresh); or cook according to package directions. Drain well.

While pasta is cooking, stir cream and lemon juice into tomato purée. Bring to a boil over high heat, stirring often; cook until sauce boils and thickens slightly (about 3 minutes).

Divide pasta among shallow bowls or rimmed plates; spoon sauce over each serving. Garnish with basil sprigs. Serve with cheese to add to taste. Makes 2 main-dish or 4 first-course servings.

Per main-dish serving: 942 calories, 25 g protein, 98 g carbohydrates, 50 g total fat, 146 mg cholesterol, 643 mg sodium

Bucatini, Amatrice Style

Preparation time: About 10 minutes

Cooking time: 20 to 25 minutes

Cooked in the manner favored in a small town north of Rome, the pasta in this classic dish is a thin, hollow tube in the shape of a drinking straw. You may find it labeled *bucatini*, *perciatelli*, or (in a thinner version) *perciatellini*.

 4 ounces sliced pancetta or bacon, cut into ½- by 1-inch strips
  Olive oil or salad oil (if needed)
 1 large onion, finely chopped
 ½ teaspoon crushed dried hot red chiles
 1 clove garlic, minced or pressed
 1 can (14½ oz.) pear-shaped tomatoes
 ⅓ cup dry white wine
 2 tablespoons chopped parsley
 8 ounces dry bucatini or other thin pasta tubes
  Salt
 ⅓ to ½ cup grated Parmesan cheese

In a wide frying pan, cook pancetta over medium heat until it is crisp and lightly browned, stirring often. Lift out, drain, and set aside. Measure the drippings; add oil, if needed, to make ¼ cup.

To drippings, add onion and chiles. Stir until onion is soft but not brown (6 to 8 minutes). Add garlic, tomatoes (break up with a spoon) and their liquid, wine, and parsley. Boil gently until slightly thickened (10 to 15 minutes); stir occasionally.

Meanwhile, in a 5- to 6-quart pan, cook bucatini in 3 quarts boiling water just until tender to bite (about 10 minutes); or cook according to package directions. Drain well and place on a deep platter.

Mix pancetta into sauce; season to taste with salt. Spoon sauce over pasta; mix lightly, using 2 forks. Serve with cheese to add to taste. Makes 2 main-dish or 4 first-course servings.

Per main-dish serving: 861 calories, 29 g protein, 102 g carbohydrates, 37 g total fat, 41 mg cholesterol, 1,006 mg sodium

Pictured on facing page

Baked Tomato Spaghetti

Preparation time: About 20 minutes

Baking time: 55 to 70 minutes

Cooking time: 10 to 12 minutes

Baked Roma-type tomatoes and fresh basil make a savory sauce for spaghetti in this Florentine first course. Long cooking partially dries the tomatoes, intensifying their sweetness.

- 12 medium-size firm-ripe pear-shaped (Roma-type) tomatoes (about 1¾ lbs. *total*)
  Salt and pepper
- 3 to 6 cloves garlic, minced
- ½ cup chopped parsley
- ½ cup olive oil
- 1 pound dry spaghetti
- 2 tablespoons butter or margarine, at room temperature
- ½ cup whole fresh basil leaves or 2 tablespoons dry basil
  Grated Parmesan cheese (optional)

Cut tomatoes in half lengthwise; set, cut sides up, in a shallow 9- by 13-inch baking pan or dish. Sprinkle lightly with salt and pepper. Mix garlic, ⅓ cup of the parsley, and 2 tablespoons of the oil; pat mixture over cut sides of tomatoes. Drizzle with 2 tablespoons more oil. Bake, uncovered, in a 425° oven until browned on top (55 to 70 minutes; pan juices may become very dark).

When tomatoes are almost done, in a 6- to 8-quart pan, cook spaghetti in 4 quarts boiling water just until tender to bite (10 to 12 minutes); or cook according to package directions.

Meanwhile, in a warm large serving bowl, place butter, remaining parsley, remaining ¼ cup oil, basil, and 4 of the baked tomato halves. Remove and discard most of the skin from the 4 halves; coarsely mash halves.

Drain spaghetti well; add to tomato mixture and mix lightly, using 2 forks. Add remaining baked tomato halves and pan juices. Mix gently; season to taste with salt and pepper. Serve with cheese, if desired. Makes 6 to 8 first-course servings.

Per serving: 434 calories, 10 g protein, 55 g carbohydrates, 20 g total fat, 9 mg cholesterol, 46 mg sodium

Wide Noodles in Tomato-Cheese Sauce

Preparation time: About 15 minutes

Cooking time: About 15 minutes

The broad egg noodles featured in this distinctive dish are called *pappardelle* in Italy; you may be able to find them in stores featuring imported foods. (If you make your own fresh pasta, just cut it half the width of lasagne.) Here, the noodles are served in a creamy tomato sauce with mozzarella—a combination the Italians call *pappardelle al telefono*, describing the way the cheese stretches out like a telephone cord when you lift the pasta.

- 2 tablespoons butter or margarine
- ⅓ cup finely chopped onion
- 2 tablespoons chopped fresh basil or 1 teaspoon dry basil
- 4 medium-size pear-shaped (Roma-type) tomatoes (about 8 oz. *total*), peeled, seeded, and chopped
- 1 clove garlic, minced or pressed
- ½ cup whipping cream
- 1 package (8½ oz.) dry pappardelle (wide fettuccine), 10 to 12 ounces fresh pappardelle, or 8 ounces dry extra-wide egg noodles
  Salt and ground white pepper
- 1 cup (4 oz.) shredded whole-milk mozzarella cheese
- ⅓ to ½ cup grated Parmesan cheese

Melt butter in a wide frying pan over medium heat. Add onion and cook, stirring occasionally, until soft but not brown (about 3 minutes). Stir in basil, tomatoes, garlic, and cream. Cook, uncovered, stirring often, until tomatoes are soft (6 to 8 minutes). Transfer to a food processor or blender; whirl until smooth. Return sauce to pan; set aside.

In a 5- to 6-quart pan, cook pasta in 3 quarts boiling water just until barely tender to bite (3 to 4 minutes for dry pappardelle, about 2 minutes for fresh pappardelle, 4 to 6 minutes for noodles); or cook according to package directions. Drain well.

Meanwhile, reheat sauce over low heat. Season to taste with salt and white pepper. Sprinkle with mozzarella cheese. Heat without stirring just until cheese is melted (about 3 minutes). Add pasta; mix lightly, using 2 spoons. Serve with Parmesan cheese to add to taste. Makes 4 first-course servings.

Per serving: 505 calories, 18 g protein, 49 g carbohydrates, 27 g total fat, 134 mg cholesterol, 338 mg sodium

Baked fresh Roma tomatoes replace the traditional slow-cooked sauce in this light, lively Baked Tomato Spaghetti (recipe on facing page). Spicy fresh basil balances the sweetness of the tomatoes.

Linguine with Zucchini

Preparation time: 12 to 15 minutes

Cooking time: 6 to 10 minutes

When time is short, try this quick entrée—*al dente* linguine topped with shredded zucchini in a two-cheese sauce.

- 3 tablespoons salad oil
- 6 medium-size zucchini (about 1½ lbs. total), coarsely shredded (5 to 6 cups)
- 3 large cloves garlic, minced or pressed
- 10 to 12 ounces fresh linguine or 8 ounces dry linguine
- ¼ cup chopped parsley
- ¼ cup butter or margarine
- ½ cup half-and-half
- ½ cup grated Parmesan cheese
- 1½ cups (6 oz.) shredded jack cheese
     Salt and freshly ground pepper

Heat oil in a wide frying pan over high heat. Add zucchini and garlic; cook, stirring, just until zucchini is tender-crisp to bite (3 to 4 minutes). Reduce heat to low.

While zucchini is cooking, in a 5- to 6-quart pan, cook linguine in 3 quarts boiling water just until tender to bite (1 to 2 minutes for fresh pasta, 8 to 10 minutes for dry); or cook according to package directions. Drain well and set aside.

To zucchini mixture, add parsley, butter, and half-and-half; stir lightly until butter is melted. Add pasta, Parmesan cheese, and jack cheese. Mix lightly, using 2 forks. Season to taste with salt and pepper. Makes 4 servings.

Per serving: 691 calories, 28 g protein, 51 g carbohydrates, 43 g total fat, 179 mg cholesterol, 572 mg sodium

■ **To Microwave:** Decrease oil to 1 tablespoon. In a 3- to 3½-quart microwave-safe casserole, mix oil, zucchini, and garlic. Microwave, covered, on **HIGH (100%)** for 5 to 6 minutes or until tender-crisp to bite, stirring 2 or 3 times. Stir in parsley, butter, and half-and-half. Microwave, covered, on **HIGH (100%)** for 2½ to 3 minutes or until butter is melted, stirring once. Meanwhile, cook and drain linguine as directed in recipe. Mix pasta and cheeses lightly into zucchini mixture; microwave, covered, on **HIGH (100%)** for 2 minutes. Let stand, covered, for 1 minute, then season to taste with salt and pepper.

Angel Hair Primavera

Preparation time: About 20 minutes

Cooking time: About 15 minutes

Green and golden spring vegetables in profusion make this delicate dish a seasonal treat.

- 8 ounces asparagus, tough ends snapped off, spears cut into bite-size pieces
- 1 medium-size or large yellow pattypan squash (4 to 6 oz.), cut into thin bite-size pieces
- 1 cup small broccoli flowerets
- 4 ounces Chinese pea pods (also called snow or sugar peas), ends and strings removed
- 2 tablespoons pine nuts
- 3 tablespoons butter or margarine
- 4 ounces mushrooms, thinly sliced
- 2 ounces thinly sliced prosciutto, cut into strips (optional)
- ¼ cup thinly sliced green onions (including tops)
- 1 clove garlic, minced or pressed
- 1 cup whipping cream
- ⅓ cup dry white wine
- ⅛ teaspoon *each* ground nutmeg and ground white pepper
- 6 ounces dry capellini or 1 package (9 oz.) fresh angel hair pasta
- ½ to ¾ cup grated Parmesan cheese

In a 3- to 4-quart pan, cook asparagus, squash, and broccoli in about 1 quart boiling water, uncovered, for 2 minutes. Add pea pods; cook just until water returns to a boil. Drain vegetables and set aside.

Stir pine nuts in a wide frying pan over medium-low heat until nuts are lightly browned (about 3 minutes), then remove from pan and set aside.

Increase heat to medium. Melt butter in pan; add mushrooms and cook, stirring, until they begin to brown (3 to 5 minutes). Add prosciutto (if used), onions, and garlic; continue to cook, stirring often, until onions are soft and bright green (1 to 2 minutes). Add cream, wine, nutmeg, and white pepper. Increase heat to high and bring to a boil; boil, stirring occasionally, for 2 minutes.

Meanwhile, in a 5- to 6-quart pan, cook pasta in 3 quarts boiling water just until tender to bite (about 3 minutes for dry pasta, 1 to 2 minutes for fresh); or cook according to package directions. Drain well.

To cream mixture, add vegetables, pine nuts, and ⅓ cup of the cheese, then stir gently just until heated through. Remove from heat. Using 2 forks, stir in pasta until lightly coated with sauce. Serve with additional cheese to add to taste. Makes about 3 main-dish or 5 first-course servings.

Per main-dish serving: 702 calories, 22 g protein, 58 g carbohydrates, 45 g total fat, 131 mg cholesterol, 431 mg sodium

The enticing aroma alone is enough to explain the magic of pesto. Fabled as the synthesis of the sunny flavors and fragrances of Liguria (the hilly coastal region near Genoa), it's actually a simple, quick-to-make paste of fresh basil, Parmesan cheese, and olive oil. In its classic version, the mixture is pulverized with a mortar and pestle—hence the name *pesto*, which means "pounded" in Italian. But a food processor or blender gets the ingredients together far more quickly and uniformly.

Taking liberties with the traditional preparation technique is just one of the ways you can vary this pungent green sauce. Many cooks wouldn't consider making pesto without garlic; others routinely add pine nuts or walnuts, toasted or plain. (To toast nuts for any of the following recipes, stir pine nuts or coarsely chopped walnuts in a frying pan over medium-low heat until lightly browned, about 3 minutes.) Another way to vary pesto is to use other fresh herbs or greens in place of or in addition to basil. To prepare the herbs or greens, rinse them well, then drain and pat dry.

To serve any of these pesto sauces with pasta, add 6 to 8 tablespoons of the pesto and ¼ cup butter or margarine (at room temperature) to 4 cups hot cooked fettuccine, spaghetti, linguine, or similar pasta. Mix lightly; serve with grated Parmesan cheese and additional pesto to add to taste.

To store pesto, refrigerate or freeze it. It will darken slightly as it stands; covering the top with a thin layer of oil will help preserve the color.

Pasta with Pesto

Classic Pesto

2 cups lightly packed fresh basil leaves
1 cup (about 5 oz.) grated Parmesan cheese
½ to ⅔ cup olive oil
1 or 2 cloves garlic (optional)

In a blender or food processor, whirl basil, cheese, ½ cup of the oil, and garlic (if used) until smoothly puréed; add more oil, if needed. If made ahead, cover and refrigerate for up to 5 days; or freeze in small portions. Makes about 1½ cups.

Per tablespoon: 79 calories, 3 g protein, 1 g carbohydrates, 7 g total fat, 5 mg cholesterol, 111 mg sodium

Basil-Cilantro Pesto

Follow directions for **Classic Pesto,** but decrease basil to 1½ cups and add ½ cup firmly packed **fresh cilantro (coriander) leaves.** Decrease cheese to ¾ cup. Increase garlic to 3 cloves. Add 2 tablespoons *each* **pine nuts** and coarsely chopped **walnuts** (toasted, if desired). Makes about 1¼ cups.

Per tablespoon: 84 calories, 2 g protein, 1 g carbohydrates, 8 g total fat, 2 mg cholesterol, 57 mg sodium

Cilantro Pesto

Follow directions for **Classic Pesto,** but omit basil; instead, use 2 cups firmly packed **fresh cilantro (coriander) leaves.** Decrease cheese to ½ cup, decrease oil to ¼ cup, and use only 1 clove garlic. Add ¼ cup **pine nuts** (toasted, if desired) and 1 teaspoon grated **lime peel;** season to taste with **salt.** Makes about ¾ cup.

Per tablespoon: 71 calories, 2 g protein, 0.6 g carbohydrates, 7 g total fat, 3 mg cholesterol, 63 mg sodium

Spinach-Herb Pesto

Follow directions for **Classic Pesto,** but omit basil; instead, use 1½ cups lightly packed **spinach leaves** and ¼ cup lightly packed **fresh tarragon, thyme, marjoram, or oregano leaves** (tough stems discarded). Decrease cheese to ½ cup. Makes about 1 cup.

Per tablespoon: 84 calories, 1 g protein, 0.4 g carbohydrates, 9 g total fat, 2 mg cholesterol, 52 mg sodium

Dried Tomato Pesto

Follow directions for **Classic Pesto,** but add ¼ cup chopped drained **dried tomatoes packed in oil.** Decrease cheese to ½ cup. Use 2 cloves garlic. Makes about 1¼ cups.

Per tablespoon: 81 calories, 1 g protein, 2 g carbohydrates, 8 g total fat, 2 mg cholesterol, 103 mg sodium

Pictured on facing page

Linguine with Morels & Asparagus

Preparation time: About 10 minutes

Soaking time: About 45 minutes

Cooking time: 12 to 15 minutes

In a spectacular gathering of gastronomic treasures, spring asparagus and flavorful morels lend elegance to golden, creamy pasta.

- ½ to 1 cup (½ to 1 oz.) dried morel mushrooms
- 12 ounces asparagus, tough ends snapped off, spears cut into 1-inch-long pieces
- 2 tablespoons pine nuts
- 3 tablespoons butter or margarine
- 2 tablespoons finely chopped shallot
- 1 cup whipping cream
- 6 ounces dry linguine or 1 package (9 oz.) fresh linguine
- 2 tablespoons 1-inch-long chive strips
- 1 teaspoon chopped fresh thyme or ¼ teaspoon dry thyme leaves
  Salt
  Chive blossoms or other small edible flower petals (optional)
- ⅓ to ½ cup grated Parmesan cheese

Place mushrooms in a medium-size bowl; cover with hot water. Let stand until soft (about 45 minutes). Drain, reserving ½ cup of the soaking liquid. Cut mushrooms lengthwise into halves or quarters; pat dry and set aside.

Steam asparagus, covered, on a rack over 1 inch of boiling water until barely tender when pierced (3 to 4 minutes). Remove asparagus from pan and set aside.

Stir pine nuts in a wide frying pan over medium-low heat until lightly browned (about 3 minutes); remove from pan and set aside. Increase heat to medium. Melt butter in pan, then add mushrooms and shallot. Cook, stirring often, until mushrooms are lightly browned (4 to 5 minutes). Add reserved ½ cup mushroom soaking liquid and cream. Increase heat to high, bring mixture to a boil, and boil, stirring often, until liquid is reduced by about a third.

Meanwhile, in a 5- to 6-quart pan, cook linguine in 3 quarts boiling water just until tender to bite (8 to 10 minutes for dry pasta, 1 to 2 minutes for fresh); or cook according to package directions. Drain well and divide among wide, shallow bowls.

To sauce, add chive strips, thyme, and asparagus; stir just until heated through. Season to taste with salt. Spoon over linguine; sprinkle with pine nuts and chive blossoms (if used). Serve with cheese to add to taste. Makes 4 first-course servings.

Per serving: 499 calories, 13 g protein, 41 g carbohydrates, 33 g total fat, 96 mg cholesterol, 270 mg sodium

Pasta with Swiss Chard

Preparation time: About 15 minutes

Cooking time: About 35 minutes

Toasted pecans, crisp bacon, and ribbons of Swiss chard dress up short tube-shaped pasta such as *penne*, *mostaccioli*, or *ziti* in this savory main course.

- 1 pound Swiss chard or kale, rinsed well
- 1 cup pecan halves
- ¾ cup (6 oz.) firmly packed chopped bacon
- 3 cloves garlic, minced or pressed
- ¼ to ½ teaspoon crushed dried hot red chiles
- 8 to 10 ounces dry small tube-shaped pasta such as penne, mostaccioli, or ziti
- 2 teaspoons Dijon mustard
- 2 tablespoons white wine vinegar
- 1½ cups (about 7½ oz.) freshly grated Parmesan or Romano cheese

Trim and discard ends of chard stems; then cut off remainder of stems at base of each leaf. Thinly slice stems and leaves, keeping them separate. (If using kale, cut off and discard coarse stems; slice leaves thinly.) Set chard or kale aside.

Stir pecans in a wide frying pan over medium heat until lightly browned (8 to 10 minutes); remove from pan and set aside. Add bacon to pan; cook, stirring often, until crisp and brown (about 10 minutes). Lift out, drain, and set aside. Discard all but 3 tablespoons of the drippings. Add chard stems, garlic, and chiles to drippings; cook, stirring often, until stems are limp (about 10 minutes). Add chard leaves (or all the kale) and stir until tender to bite (about 5 minutes).

Meanwhile, in a 5- to 6-quart pan, cook pasta in 3 quarts boiling water just until tender to bite (10 to 12 minutes); or cook according to package directions. Drain well.

In a warm large serving bowl, combine pasta, mustard, and vinegar. Using 2 spoons, lightly mix in cheese, then greens and bacon. Sprinkle with pecans. Makes 4 to 6 servings.

Per serving: 767 calories, 31 g protein, 57 g carbohydrates, 47 g total fat, 54 mg cholesterol, 1,212 mg sodium

Among the most aromatic and full-flavored of wild mushrooms, crinkly morels perfume creamy Linguine with Morels & Asparagus (recipe on facing page). You'll find the morels in specialty food markets.

Linguine with Double Mushroom Sauce

Preparation time: About 10 minutes

Cooking time: About 20 minutes

To make this stylish first course, combine familiar brown or white button mushrooms with one or more unusual, subtly flavored varieties, such as shiitake or oyster mushrooms or angel trumpets.

> 8 ounces mushrooms (choose 2 or 3 different kinds; see suggestions in recipe introduction above)
>
> ⅓ cup olive oil
>
> 1 clove garlic, minced or pressed
>
> ½ cup dry white wine
>
> 1 package (9 oz.) fresh linguine or 6 ounces dry linguine
>
> 1 small pear-shaped (Roma-type) tomato (about 1½ oz.), seeded and finely chopped
>
> ¼ cup chopped Italian (flat-leaf) parsley
> Salt and freshly ground pepper

Cut any large mushrooms into quarters or halves. Heat oil in a wide frying pan over medium heat. Add mushrooms and cook, stirring often, until they begin to brown (about 10 minutes). Stir in garlic. Add wine, bring to a boil, and boil gently until liquid is reduced by about half (3 to 5 minutes).

Meanwhile, in a 5- to 6-quart pan, cook linguine in 3 quarts boiling water just until tender to bite (1 to 2 minutes for fresh pasta, 8 to 10 minutes for dry); or cook according to package directions. Drain pasta well.

Stir tomato and parsley into mushroom mixture just until heated through (about 1 minute). Season to taste with salt and pepper. Remove from heat and add pasta. Mix lightly, using 2 spoons. Makes 4 first-course servings.

Per serving: 362 calories, 9 g protein, 39 g carbohydrates, 20 g total fat, 75 mg cholesterol, 24 mg sodium

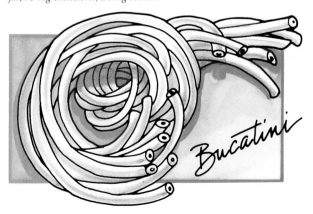

Bucatini

Tortellini with Mushroom-Cheese Sauce

Preparation time: About 15 minutes

Cooking time: 15 to 20 minutes

Start with ready-made tortellini, fresh, frozen, or dried—then add a garlic-and basil-accented mushroom sauce, mellowed with cream cheese.

> 1 package (12 oz.) frozen tortellini, 12 ounces fresh tortellini, or 1 package (7 or 8 oz.) dry tortellini
>
> 1 tablespoon butter or margarine
>
> 1 pound mushrooms, finely chopped
>
> 3 cloves garlic, minced or pressed
>
> 1 tablespoon minced fresh basil leaves or ½ teaspoon dry basil
>
> 2 small packages (3 oz. *each*) cream cheese
>
> ¾ cup milk
> Parsley sprigs

In a 5- to 6-quart pan, cook tortellini in 3 quarts boiling water just until tender to bite (15 to 20 minutes for frozen tortellini, 4 to 6 minutes for fresh, 15 to 20 minutes for dry); or cook according to package directions. Drain well.

While tortellini are cooking, melt butter in a wide frying pan over medium-high heat. Add mushrooms, garlic, and basil; cook, stirring often, until all liquid has evaporated and mushrooms are beginning to brown (10 to 12 minutes). Add cream cheese and milk; stir until cheese is melted and sauce comes to a gentle boil.

Remove sauce from heat, add tortellini, and mix lightly, using 2 spoons. Garnish with parsley. Makes 4 main-dish or 6 first-course servings.

Per main-dish serving: 486 calories, 21 g protein, 43 g carbohydrates, 26 g total fat, 61 mg cholesterol, 479 mg sodium

Fettuccine Emmenthaler

Preparation time: About 5 minutes

Cooking time: 3 to 4 minutes

This refined version of pasta and cheese makes a satisfying main dish; serve it with your favorite green vegetable.

10 ounces fresh thin fettuccine or 8 ounces dry thin fettuccine

½ cup (¼ lb.) butter or margarine, melted

2 cups (8 oz.) shredded Emmenthaler or Swiss cheese

Freshly ground pepper

Chopped parsley

In a 5- to 6-quart pan, cook fettuccine in 3 quarts boiling water just until tender to bite (3 to 4 minutes for fresh pasta, 7 to 8 minutes for dry); or cook according to package directions. Drain well; transfer to a wide bowl or deep platter.

Immediately add butter and 1 cup of the cheese to hot pasta; rapidly lift pasta with 2 forks to blend in melting cheese. Sprinkle on remaining 1 cup cheese a little at a time, lifting pasta to mix in well. Sprinkle with pepper and parsley. Makes 4 servings.

Per serving: 622 calories, 25 g protein, 41 g carbohydrates, 40 g total fat, 198 mg cholesterol, 401 mg sodium

Capellini with Broccoli Cream Sauce

Preparation time: 10 to 15 minutes

Cooking time: About 10 minutes

Serve this simple but luxurious pasta dish with crisp bread sticks and an Italian white wine, such as pinot grigio or soave.

1½ pounds broccoli

1 package (10 oz.) dry capellini or coil vermicelli

6 tablespoons butter or margarine

⅓ cup water

2 cups whipping cream

¼ teaspoon ground nutmeg

2 cups (about 10 oz.) freshly grated Parmesan cheese

Trim and discard tough ends from broccoli stalks. Peel stems; finely chop broccoli, reserving a few whole flowerets for garnish. Set aside.

In a 5- to 6-quart pan, cook capellini in 3 quarts boiling water just until tender to bite (about 3 minutes); or cook according to package directions. Drain, rinse with cold water, and drain well again.

Melt butter in a wide frying pan over medium-high heat; add all broccoli and ⅓ cup water. Cover and cook until broccoli is tender when pierced (about 5 minutes); remove flowerets from pan and set aside.

Add cream and nutmeg to remaining broccoli in pan; bring to a boil, then add pasta. Cook, mixing lightly with 2 spoons, just until mixture is hot and cream clings to pasta. Remove from heat, sprinkle with 1¼ cups of the cheese, and mix lightly again.

Transfer pasta to a warm deep platter. Sprinkle with 3 to 4 tablespoons more cheese and garnish with broccoli flowerets. Serve with remaining cheese to add to taste. Makes 6 servings.

Per serving: 714 calories, 27 g protein, 43 g carbohydrates, 49 g total fat, 152 mg cholesterol, 921 mg sodium

Lasagne Packets

Preparation time: About 10 minutes

Baking time: 10 to 15 minutes

Instant lasagne, a dry pasta product that needs only brief moistening to be ready to use, speeds up the preparation of this hearty baked entrée.

4 to 6 sheets (*each* about 7 inches square) instant lasagne noodles

1 package (10 oz.) frozen chopped spinach, thawed

2 cloves garlic, minced or pressed

1 teaspoon Italian herb seasoning or ¼ teaspoon *each* dry basil and dry oregano, thyme, and marjoram leaves

1½ cups prepared (refrigerated or bottled) pasta sauce, such as marinara, Bolognese, roasted red pepper, or shrimp sauce

1 pound ricotta or small-curd cottage cheese

½ cup grated Parmesan, Romano, or Asiago cheese

Pour 2 quarts hottest tap water into a 5- to 6-quart pan. Add lasagne and let stand until pliable (about 5 minutes).

Meanwhile, squeeze as much liquid as possible from spinach. In a bowl, mix spinach, garlic, herb seasoning, ½ cup of the pasta sauce, ricotta cheese, and ¼ cup of the Parmesan cheese.

Drain lasagne sheets well, then place on a flat surface. Scoop an equal amount of spinach mixture onto center of each. Fold all 4 corners of each sheet to center over filling, pulling corners together to make snug packets. Set packets, folded sides down, in a greased 9- by 13-inch baking dish. Moisten tops of packets evenly with remaining 1 cup sauce; sprinkle with remaining ¼ cup Parmesan cheese.

Bake, uncovered, in a 400° oven until packets are heated through; cut to test (10 to 15 minutes). Makes 4 to 6 servings.

Per serving: 305 calories, 20 g protein, 31 g carbohydrates, 11 g total fat, 34 mg cholesterol, 533 mg sodium

A favorite pasta from Italy's Adriatic coast, cup-shaped orecchiette are perfectly designed to hold sauces and seasonings. In Orecchiette with Spinach & Garlic (recipe on facing page), they gain emphatic flavor from olive oil that's scented with garlic and piqued with hot chiles.

Vegetable Lasagne

Preparation time: About 25 minutes

Cooking time: About 20 minutes

Baking time: About 25 minutes; 50 minutes if refrigerated

All the hearty flavor of a classic lasagne, but none of the meat! This bright, fresh version features a variety of vegetables and a trio of cheeses.

   8 ounces dry lasagne
   4 large carrots (about 12 oz. *total*), cut into ¼-inch-thick slices
   3 large zucchini (about 1 lb. *total*), cut into ¼-inch-thick slices
   2 tablespoons olive oil or salad oil
   1 medium-size onion, finely chopped
   8 ounces mushrooms, thinly sliced
   1 teaspoon *each* dry basil, thyme leaves, and oregano leaves
   1 jar (32 oz.) marinara sauce
   2 packages (10 oz. *each*) frozen chopped spinach, thawed
   8 ounces ricotta cheese
   3 cups (12 oz.) shredded mozzarella cheese
   ¼ cup grated Parmesan cheese

In a 5- to 6-quart pan, cook lasagne and carrots in 3 quarts boiling water for 6 minutes. Add zucchini; continue to cook just until lasagne is tender to bite (4 to 5 more minutes). Drain well; set lasagne and vegetables aside separately.

In same pan, heat oil over high heat; add onion, mushrooms, basil, thyme, and oregano. Cook, stirring often, until onion is soft and all liquid has evaporated (5 to 8 minutes). Remove from heat, stir in marinara sauce, and set aside.

Squeeze as much liquid as possible from spinach. Mix spinach and ricotta cheese; set aside.

Spread a third of the sauce in a shallow 2½- to 3-quart baking dish. Arrange half the lasagne over sauce. Add half each of the blanched carrots and zucchini, spinach mixture, and mozzarella cheese. Repeat layers, using half the remaining sauce and all the remaining lasagne, carrots, zucchini, spinach mixture, and mozzarella. Spread remaining sauce on top, then sprinkle with Parmesan cheese. (At this point, you may cover baking dish and refrigerate for up to a day.)

Set baking dish in a shallow rimmed baking pan to catch any drips. Bake, uncovered, until hot in center. Bake freshly made lasagne in a 400° oven for about 25 minutes; bake refrigerated lasagne in a 350° oven for about 50 minutes. Let stand for about 5 minutes before serving. To serve, cut into squares. Makes 6 servings.

Per serving: 586 calories, 29 g protein, 63 g carbohydrates, 27 g total fat, 59 mg cholesterol, 1,367 mg sodium

Pictured on facing page

Orecchiette with Spinach & Garlic

Preparation time: 15 to 20 minutes

Cooking time: About 15 minutes

Some people see fanciful shapes in clouds, but Italians find them in pasta. You might take round, shallow *orecchiette* for diminutive berets, but their Italian name indicates that they're meant to be seen as little ears.

   2 bunches (about 12 oz. *each*) spinach, rinsed well and drained
  12 ounces dry orecchiette or ruote (wheel-shaped pasta)
   ⅓ cup olive oil
   6 cloves garlic, minced or pressed
   ½ teaspoon crushed dried hot red chiles
     Salt
   ⅓ to ½ cup grated Parmesan cheese

Remove and discard spinach stems; chop leaves coarsely and set aside.

In a 6- to 8-quart pan, cook orecchiette in 4 quarts boiling water just until tender to bite (12 to 15 minutes); or cook according to package directions. Just before pasta is done, stir in spinach. Cook, uncovered, stirring to distribute spinach, just until water returns to a full boil. Drain pasta and spinach.

While pasta is cooking, heat oil in a wide frying pan over medium heat. Stir in garlic and chiles. Cook, uncovered, until garlic turns opaque (about 2 minutes). Add pasta and spinach to pan; mix lightly, using 2 spoons. Season to taste with salt. Serve with cheese to add to taste. Makes 6 first-course servings.

Per serving: 363 calories, 12 g protein, 47 g carbohydrates, 15 g total fat, 4 mg cholesterol, 170 mg sodium

Pasta with Peppers & Onions

Preparation time: About 20 minutes

Cooking time: About 30 minutes

Your choice of red, yellow, or orange bell peppers enlivens a creamy, walnut-sprinkled sauce for fettuccine. (For an especially eye-catching entrée, you might combine all three colors of peppers.)

- ¼ **cup butter or margarine**
- ⅓ **cup coarsely chopped walnuts**
- 2 **large onions, thinly sliced**
- 3 **medium-size red, yellow, or orange bell peppers (about 1 lb. *total*), seeded and cut into ¼-inch-wide strips**
- 8 **ounces dry fettuccine or 10 to 12 ounces fresh fettuccine**
- ½ **cup *each* regular-strength chicken broth and whipping cream**
- ⅛ **teaspoon ground nutmeg**
- ½ **cup grated Parmesan cheese**
  Salt and pepper

Melt 1 tablespoon of the butter in a wide frying pan over medium-low heat. Add walnuts and cook, stirring often, until lightly toasted (about 2 minutes). Lift out and set aside. Add remaining 3 tablespoons butter, onions, and bell peppers to pan; cook, stirring often, until onions are very soft and light golden (20 to 25 minutes).

Meanwhile, in a 5- to 6-quart pan, cook fettuccine in 3 quarts boiling water just until tender to bite (8 to 10 minutes for dry pasta, 3 to 4 minutes for fresh); drain well.

To bell pepper mixture, add broth, cream, and nutmeg. Increase heat to high and bring to a full boil. Reduce heat to low; add fettuccine and cheese. Mix lightly, using 2 forks. Season to taste with salt and pepper, then sprinkle with walnuts. Makes 4 servings.

Per serving: 570 calories, 15 g protein, 54 g carbohydrates, 33 g total fat, 125 mg cholesterol, 447 mg sodium

Orecchiette

Garbanzo Pasta

Preparation time: 10 to 15 minutes

Cooking time: 10 to 12 minutes

You can put this spirited main dish together in a hurry, using ingredients you probably already have on hand in the pantry and refrigerator.

- 8 **ounces dry spaghetti**
- 4 **ounces sliced bacon (about 5 slices), cut into ½-inch pieces**
- 3 **tablespoons olive oil or salad oil**
- 1 **medium-size onion, finely chopped**
- 3 **cloves garlic, minced or pressed**
- 1 **can (15 oz.) garbanzo beans, drained**
- ¾ **cup regular-strength beef broth**
- ¼ **teaspoon crushed dried hot red chiles**
- ½ **cup finely chopped parsley**
- ½ **cup grated Parmesan cheese**

In a 5- to 6-quart pan, cook spaghetti in 3 quarts boiling water just until tender to bite (10 to 12 minutes); or cook according to package directions. Drain well.

While spaghetti is cooking, in a wide frying pan, cook bacon over medium heat until crisp. Lift out, drain, and set aside. Discard all but 2 tablespoons of the drippings. Add oil, onion, and garlic to drippings. Cook, stirring often, until onion is soft but not brown (about 5 minutes). Add garbanzos, broth, chiles, and parsley. With a spoon, mash garbanzos slightly. Bring to a boil, then add pasta. Mix lightly, using 2 spoons, until pasta is hot.

Transfer pasta mixture to a serving dish. Sprinkle with cheese and mix lightly. Sprinkle with bacon. Makes 4 servings.

Per serving: 583 calories, 20 g protein, 71 g carbohydrates, 24 g total fat, 19 mg cholesterol, 823 mg sodium

■ ***To Microwave:*** Cook pasta as directed in recipe. Place bacon pieces in a single layer on several layers of paper towels; cover with another paper towel. Microwave on **HIGH (100%)** for 4 to 5 minutes or until bacon is brown; set aside. In a 3- to 3½-quart microwave-safe casserole, combine oil, onion, and garlic. Microwave, covered, on **HIGH (100%)** for 4 to 5 minutes or until onion is soft, stirring once or twice. Add garbanzos, broth, chiles, and parsley; mash garbanzos slightly with a spoon. Microwave, covered, on **HIGH (100%)** for 3½ to 5 minutes or until mixture is hot and bubbling, stirring once. Mix in pasta, cover, and let stand for 1 minute. Sprinkle with Parmesan cheese and mix lightly; then sprinkle with bacon.

Tagliarini with Chèvre & Olives

Preparation time: About 15 minutes

Cooking time: 12 to 15 minutes

Cream, chicken broth, and distinctively flavored goat cheese mingle in a rich sauce for tagliarini. Crisp pine nuts and tangy olives accent the dish.

- ¼ **cup pine nuts**
- 2 **cups** *each* **whipping cream and regular-strength chicken broth**
- 8 **to 12 ounces soft, unripened chèvre (trimmed of coating, if necessary)**
- ½ **cup Spanish-style or Niçoise olives, pitted and chopped**
- 8 **ounces dry tagliarini or 10 to 12 ounces fresh tagliarini**
- ¼ **cup butter or margarine, melted**
- 1 **tablespoon grated orange peel**
- 3 **tablespoons chopped chives**
  Whole chives

Stir pine nuts in a medium-size frying pan over medium-low heat until lightly browned (about 3 minutes); set aside.

In a 4- to 5-quart pan, combine cream and broth. Bring to a boil over high heat; boil, uncovered, stirring occasionally, until reduced to 1½ cups. Reduce heat to low and whisk in about half of the cheese, adding enough to develop a rich cheese flavor; stir in olives and keep warm.

Meanwhile, in a 5- to 6-quart pan, cook tagliarini in 3 quarts boiling water just until tender to bite (6 to 7 minutes for dry pasta, 2 to 3 minutes for fresh); or cook according to package directions. Drain well, then return to pan over low heat. Add pine nuts, butter, and 2 teaspoons of the orange peel. Mix lightly, using 2 forks.

Pour sauce into a warm serving bowl; mound pasta in center. Crumble remaining cheese and sprinkle over pasta with chopped chives and remaining 1 teaspoon orange peel. Garnish with whole chives. Makes 6 first-course servings.

Per serving: 668 calories, 18 g protein, 36 g carbohydrates, 52 g total fat, 153 mg cholesterol, 1,004 mg sodium

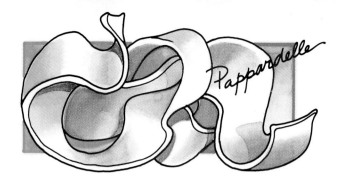

Red, White & Green Pasta

Preparation time: About 10 minutes

Cooking time: 30 to 35 minutes

Display the three colors of the Italian flag in this mellow dish. Sautéed white onions and red bell peppers are moistened with broth and lemon juice, then served over green fettuccine.

- 1 **tablespoon butter or margarine**
- 1 **tablespoon salad oil**
- 2 **large onions, thinly sliced**
- 1 **clove garlic, minced or pressed**
- 2 **large red bell peppers (about 1 lb.** *total***), seeded and cut into thin strips**
- 8 **ounces dry green fettuccine or 10 to 12 ounces fresh green fettuccine**
- ⅓ **cup regular-strength chicken or beef broth**
- 1 **tablespoon lemon juice**
  Salt and freshly ground pepper
- ¼ **cup chopped fresh basil**
- ½ **to ¾ cup grated Parmesan cheese**

Melt butter in oil in a wide frying pan over medium-low heat. Stir in onions and garlic; cook, stirring often, until onions are very soft and light golden (20 to 25 minutes). Increase heat to medium, add bell peppers, and cook, stirring often, until peppers are just limp (8 to 10 minutes).

Meanwhile, in a 5- to 6-quart pan, cook fettuccine in 3 quarts boiling water just until tender to bite (8 to 10 minutes for dry pasta, 3 to 4 minutes for fresh); or cook according to package directions. Drain well, transfer to a warm bowl or deep platter, and keep warm.

Add broth and lemon juice to onion mixture; increase heat to high and bring to a boil. Season to taste with salt and pepper. Stir in basil. Spoon sauce in a broad stripe down center of pasta; using 2 forks, mix lightly at the table. Serve with cheese to add to taste. Makes 4 to 6 first-course servings.

Per serving: 270 calories, 12 g protein, 33 g carbohydrates, 10 g total fat, 66 mg cholesterol, 319 mg sodium

Pictured on facing page

Pasta Pilaf

Preparation time: About 10 minutes

Cooking time: About 20 minutes

For a side dish that's delicious with grilled fish or roast chicken, dress tiny rice-shaped pasta with a creamy tomato sauce. You'll find the pasta labeled *orzo, riso,* or *seme di melone.*

  - 2 **tablespoons butter or margarine**
  - 1 **large onion, finely chopped**
  - 1 **large clove garlic, minced or pressed**
  - 2 **medium-size tomatoes (about 10 oz. *total*), peeled, seeded, and chopped**
  - 1 **teaspoon dry basil**
  - ¼ **cup water**
  - 1 **cup (about 8 oz.) dry rice-shaped pasta**
  - ¾ **cup frozen peas**
  - ½ **cup whipping cream**
  - ½ **to ⅔ cup grated Parmesan cheese**
    Salt and pepper

Melt butter in a wide frying pan over medium heat. Add onion and garlic; cook, stirring occasionally, until onion is soft but not brown (5 to 7 minutes). Add tomatoes, basil, and ¼ cup water; reduce heat, cover, and simmer for 10 minutes.

Meanwhile, in a 5- to 6-quart pan, cook pasta in 3 quarts boiling water just until tender to bite (about 10 minutes); or cook according to package directions. Drain well.

Add peas and cream to tomato mixture. Increase heat to high and bring to a boil; mix in pasta. Remove from heat and stir in ¼ cup of the cheese. Season to taste with salt and pepper. Serve with remaining cheese to add to taste. Makes 4 to 6 side-dish servings.

Per serving: 361 calories, 12 g protein, 43 g carbohydrates, 16 g total fat, 46 mg cholesterol, 261 mg sodium

■ ***To Microwave:*** In a 3-quart microwave-safe casserole, combine butter, onion, and garlic. Microwave, covered, on **HIGH (100%)** for 4 to 5 minutes or until onion is soft, stirring 2 or 3 times. Stir in tomatoes, basil, and 2 tablespoons water. Microwave, covered, on **HIGH (100%)** for 8 to 10 minutes or until tomatoes are very soft, stirring twice. Meanwhile, cook pasta as directed in recipe. Add peas and cream to tomato mixture. Microwave, uncovered, on **HIGH (100%)** for 3 to 4 minutes or until mixture comes to a boil. Stir in pasta, cover, and let stand for 2 minutes. Stir in ¼ cup of the cheese; season to taste with salt and pepper. Serve with remaining cheese to add to taste.

Toasted Cabbage with Noodles

Preparation time: About 15 minutes

Cooking time: 35 to 40 minutes

Wide egg noodles mingle with buttery cabbage and onions in this homey, old-fashioned side dish. It's a good accompaniment for a juicy pork roast.

  - 1 **small head green cabbage (about 1½ lbs.)**
  - ½ **cup (¼ lb.) butter or margarine**
  - 1 **large onion, finely chopped**
  - 1 **clove garlic, minced or pressed**
  - 2 **tablespoons sugar**
  - 8 **ounces dry wide egg noodles**
    Salt and pepper

Cut cabbage into fine shreds, discarding core; you should have about 2 quarts. Set aside.

Melt butter in a wide frying pan over medium heat. Add onion and garlic and cook, stirring occasionally, until onion is soft but not brown (5 to 7 minutes). Add cabbage; continue to cook, stirring often, until cabbage is softened and turns a brighter green (about 5 minutes). Sprinkle with sugar; continue to cook, stirring often, until cabbage takes on an amber color and begins to brown lightly (about 25 more minutes).

Shortly before cabbage is done, in a 5- to 6-quart pan, cook noodles in 3 quarts boiling water just until tender to bite (7 to 9 minutes); or cook according to package directions. Drain well.

In a wide, shallow serving bowl or deep platter, combine noodles and cabbage mixture; mix lightly, using 2 forks. Season to taste with salt and pepper. Makes 4 to 6 side-dish servings.

Per serving: 397 calories, 8 g protein, 46 g carbohydrates, 21 g total fat, 92 mg cholesterol, 210 mg sodium

Enfolded in a creamy fresh tomato sauce and mixed
with bright green peas, rice-shaped orzo is transformed
into a Pasta Pilaf (recipe on facing page)—an ideal
accent for an unadorned main dish such as roast
chicken or broiled fish steaks.

Pasta of a different persuasion, spaghetti squash (with pulp that naturally separates into slender strands) and zucchini (cut into long, slim ribbons) can be fanciful stand-ins for vermicelli or linguine. Top them with sauces and butters designed to complement their mild flavor and tender-crisp texture.

To bake a 2- to 3-pound spaghetti squash, pierce it in several places with a fork, then place it in a rimmed baking pan. Bake, uncovered, in a 350° oven until shell gives when pressed (1¼ to 1½ hours; turn squash after 45 minutes). Keep warm until ready to serve.

To microwave a 2- to 3-pound spaghetti squash, cut it in half lengthwise; scrape out and discard seeds. Place squash halves, cut sides up, in a 9- by 13-inch microwave-safe baking dish. Cover with plastic wrap. Microwave on **HIGH (100%)** for 15 to 20 minutes or until squash is tender when pierced, rotating each piece a half-turn after 5 minutes. Let stand, covered, for 5 minutes.

Spaghetti Squash with Turkey Sauce

- 1 spaghetti squash (2 to 3 lbs.)
- 1 pound ground turkey
- 1 medium-size red or green bell pepper (about 5 oz.), seeded and diced
- 4 ounces mushrooms, thinly sliced
- 1 can (4 oz.) diced green chiles
- 1 jar (about 15 oz.) spaghetti sauce
- ½ teaspoon Italian herb seasoning or ⅛ teaspoon *each* dry basil and dry oregano, thyme, and marjoram leaves
  Salt and ground red pepper (cayenne)
  About ¾ cup grated Parmesan cheese

Great Pretenders:
Vegetables as Pasta

Bake or microwave squash as directed at left. Meanwhile, crumble turkey into a wide frying pan; cook over medium-high heat, stirring, until pink color is almost gone. Add bell pepper and mushrooms; cook, stirring often, until mushrooms are lightly browned (about 10 minutes). Stir in chiles, spaghetti sauce, and herb seasoning. Season to taste with salt and red pepper. Reduce heat and boil gently, uncovered, for 8 to 10 minutes.

Cut baked squash in half; scrape out and discard seeds.

Loosen squash strands with a fork and scoop out onto a warm rimmed platter. Spoon sauce over squash. Serve with cheese to add to taste. Makes 6 servings.

Per serving: 305 calories, 21 g protein, 24 g carbohydrates, 15 g total fat, 59 mg cholesterol, 749 mg sodium

Spaghetti Squash Lasagne

- 2 spaghetti squash (about 2 lbs. *each*)
- 1 pound lean ground beef
- 1 clove garlic, minced or pressed
- 4 ounces mushrooms, sliced
- 1½ teaspoons dry basil
- 1½ teaspoons Italian herb seasoning or ½ teaspoon *each* dry basil, dry oregano leaves, and dry thyme or marjoram leaves
- ½ teaspoon salt
- 1 can (15 oz.) tomato purée
- ½ cup dry red wine or water
- 3 medium-size zucchini (about 12 oz. *total*), shredded
- 4 cups (1 lb.) shredded Cheddar cheese
- ½ to ¾ cup grated Parmesan cheese

Bake or microwave squash as directed at left. Meanwhile, crumble beef into a wide frying pan; cook over medium heat, stirring, until browned. Spoon off and discard fat. Add garlic and mushrooms; cook, stirring, until mushrooms are soft. Stir in basil, herb seasoning, salt, tomato purée, and wine. Reduce heat and boil gently, uncovered, for 10 to 15 minutes.

Cut baked squash in half; scrape out and discard seeds.

Loosen squash strands with a fork. Place strands from one whole squash in a greased shallow 3-quart baking dish. Lightly mix zucchini and Cheddar cheese; spoon half the mixture over squash. Cover with half the meat sauce. Repeat layers, using remaining spaghetti squash, zucchini mixture, and meat sauce.

Bake, covered, in a 350° oven until hot and bubbly (about 30 minutes). Serve with Parmesan cheese to add to taste. Makes 6 servings.

Per serving: 579 calories, 39 g protein, 19 g carbohydrates, 39 g total fat, 130 mg cholesterol, 1,163 mg sodium

Spaghetti Squash with Lime-Basil Sauce

1 spaghetti squash (2 to 3 lbs.)
1 quart lightly packed fresh basil leaves
½ cup olive oil or salad oil
2 cups (about 10 oz.) grated Parmesan cheese
2 tablespoons sugar
3 cloves garlic, quartered
¼ cup lime juice

Bake or microwave squash as directed on facing page. Meanwhile, in a blender or food processor, combine basil, oil, 1 cup of the cheese, sugar, garlic, and lime juice. Whirl until smoothly puréed. Set mixture aside.

Cut baked squash in half; scrape out and discard seeds.

Loosen squash strands with a fork and scoop out into a warm serving bowl. Add basil sauce and mix lightly, using 2 forks. Serve with remaining cheese to add to taste. Makes about 6 side-dish servings.

Per serving: 473 calories, 23 g protein, 25 g carbohydrates, 33 g total fat, 37 mg cholesterol, 909 mg sodium

Onion-Dill Spaghetti Squash

1 spaghetti squash (2 to 3 lbs.)
¼ cup butter or margarine
2 medium-size onions, coarsely chopped
1 teaspoon dill seeds
2 tablespoons vinegar
1 cup sour cream
2 small zucchini (about 6 oz. total), coarsely shredded

Bake or microwave squash as directed on facing page. Meanwhile, melt butter in a wide frying pan over medium heat. Add onions and dill seeds; cook, stirring often, until onions are very soft and light golden (about 20 minutes). Stir in vinegar and sour cream. Remove from heat and keep warm.

Cut baked squash in half; scrape out and discard seeds.

Loosen squash strands with a fork and scoop out into frying pan with onion mixture; add zucchini. Place over medium heat and mix lightly, using 2 spoons, just until heated through. Makes 4 to 6 side-dish servings.

Per serving: 255 calories, 4 g protein, 18 g carbohydrates, 20 g total fat, 45 mg cholesterol, 148 mg sodium

Zucchini Spaghetti with Veal Sauce

Savory Veal Sauce (recipe follows)
8 large zucchini (about 3 lbs. *total*)
¼ cup salad oil
3 large cloves garlic, minced or pressed
1 to 2 tablespoons butter or margarine, at room temperature
Pepper
½ to ¾ cup grated Parmesan cheese

Prepare Savory Veal Sauce. Meanwhile, using a knife or Oriental shredder, cut zucchini into long, very thin slivers (if using shredder, draw zucchini full length across coarse shredding blade).

Heat 2 tablespoons of the oil in a wide frying pan over medium-high heat. Add half each of the zucchini and garlic. Cook, lifting and gently stirring with 1 or 2 wide spatulas, just until tender-crisp to bite (3 to 4 minutes). Mound zucchini in the center of a deep platter; keep warm.

Heat remaining 2 tablespoons oil in pan; cook remaining zucchini and garlic and add to zucchini mixture on platter. Top with butter; season to taste with pepper.

Spoon sauce around but not over zucchini. Serve with cheese to add to taste. Makes 4 servings.

Savory Veal Sauce. In a wide frying pan, combine 1 tablespoon **olive oil;** 1 small **onion,** finely chopped; ½ cup finely chopped **green bell pepper;** 1 medium-size **carrot** (about 2 oz.), finely shredded; 3 **mushrooms,** thinly sliced; 1 tablespoon chopped **parsley;** 1 clove **garlic** (minced or pressed); 1 teaspoon **dry basil;** and ½ teaspoon *each* **dry rosemary** and **dry oregano leaves.** Cook over medium-high heat, stirring often, until onion is soft (about 5 minutes).

Crumble 1 pound **ground veal** or lean ground beef into pan and cook, stirring often, until lightly browned. Add 1 large can (28 oz.) **pear-shaped tomatoes** (break up with a spoon) and their liquid, 1 can (6 oz.) **tomato paste,** ⅓ cup **dry red wine,** and 1 **dry bay leaf;** bring to a boil. Adjust heat so mixture boils gently; cook, stirring occasionally, until sauce is thickened (about 20 minutes).

Season sauce to taste with **salt** and **pepper.** Discard bay leaf.

Per serving: 572 calories, 36 g protein, 34 g carbohydrates, 35 g total fat, 116 mg cholesterol, 1,072 mg sodium

Fresh dill punctuates the vodka-enhanced
sauce that swathes Penne with Smoked Salmon
(recipe on facing page). To serve this distinctive pasta
dish as an entrée, add a salad of mixed greens
and a whole-grain bread.

Seafood

As accomplices in delicious dining, pasta and seafood are perfect partners. The muted flavor of pasta balances and enhances—but never overpowers—the delicacy of fish and shellfish. For examples of this subtle sophistication, sample such combinations as Penne with Smoked Salmon, Fettuccine with Calamari, and Angel Hair with Shrimp & Mint Butter Sauce.

Another acknowledged advantage of the pasta-seafood alliance is the thriftiness pasta brings to the match. Hearty, satisfying dishes like Grilled Swordfish with Stir-fried Noodles and Barbecued Crab with Spaghetti vividly demonstrate pasta's renowned ability to stretch far costlier ingredients.

Pictured on facing page

Penne with Smoked Salmon

Preparation time: About 10 minutes

Cooking time: 10 to 12 minutes

Vodka emphasizes the flavor of a creamy, tomato-dotted sauce for silken smoked salmon and pasta tubes. Serve the dish as a first course, or present it as the entrée with tender-crisp green beans and a simple salad.

12 ounces dry small tube-shaped pasta such as penne, mostaccioli, or ziti

2 tablespoons olive oil

1 small shallot, thinly sliced

4 small pear-shaped (Roma-type) tomatoes (about 6 oz. *total*), peeled, seeded, and chopped

⅔ cup whipping cream
Pinch of ground nutmeg

2 tablespoons chopped fresh dill or ½ teaspoon dry dill weed

⅓ cup vodka

4 to 6 ounces sliced smoked salmon or lox, cut into bite-size strips
Ground white pepper
Fresh dill sprigs

In a 6- to 8-quart pan, cook pasta in 4 quarts boiling water just until tender to bite (10 to 12 minutes); or cook according to package directions. Drain well.

While pasta is cooking, heat oil in a wide frying pan over medium-low heat. Add shallot and cook, stirring often, until soft but not brown (about 3 minutes). Stir in chopped tomatoes, cover, and simmer for 5 minutes. Add cream, nutmeg, chopped dill, and vodka. Increase heat to high and bring to a full boil; boil for 1 minute.

Add pasta to sauce and mix lightly, using 2 spoons, until pasta is well coated. Remove from heat, add salmon, and mix lightly. Season to taste with white pepper and garnish with dill sprigs. Makes 4 servings.

Per serving: 541 calories, 18 g protein, 67 g carbohydrates, 22 g total fat, 53 mg cholesterol, 297 mg sodium

Tuna Carbonara

Preparation time: About 15 minutes

Cooking time: 10 to 12 minutes

This colorful dish is a good choice for a spur-of-the-moment supper. The cooked vermicelli is coated with beaten egg, helping the cheese, bell pepper strips, and tuna to cling to it.

    8 ounces dry vermicelli (not coil vermicelli)
    2 tablespoons olive oil
    2 tablespoons butter or margarine
    1 large red bell pepper (about 8 oz.), seeded and cut into thin bite-size strips
    3 cloves garlic, minced or pressed
    1 can (9¼ oz.) chunk-style tuna, drained
    4 eggs, beaten until blended
    1 cup (about 5 oz.) grated Parmesan cheese
    ¼ cup chopped parsley
       Salt and pepper

In a 5- to 6-quart pan, cook vermicelli in 3 quarts boiling water just until tender to bite (8 to 10 minutes); or cook according to package directions. Drain well.

While pasta is cooking, heat oil and butter in a wide frying pan over medium-high heat. Add bell pepper and garlic; cook, stirring often, until pepper is soft (6 to 8 minutes).

Add vermicelli and tuna to frying pan; mix lightly, using 2 forks, just until mixture is heated through. Remove from heat; then add eggs, cheese, and parsley. Mix lightly, lifting with 2 forks, until pasta is well coated with sauce. Season to taste with salt and pepper. Makes 4 servings.

Per serving: 653 calories, 45 g protein, 48 g carbohydrates, 30 g total fat, 282 mg cholesterol, 1,024 mg sodium

Fresh Tuna Puttanesca

Preparation time: About 15 minutes

Cooking time: About 20 minutes

Grilled tuna stars in a savory dish that's just right for a summer evening. In Italian cooking, *gnocchi*—the pasta specified—are usually little dumplings made from semolina or mashed potatoes. This entrée, though, uses dry gnocchi—fluted shapes rather like large shells, with ridges and hollows that are perfect for holding the fresh tomato sauce.

    5 tablespoons olive oil
    1 medium-size onion, thinly sliced
    1 teaspoon crushed dried hot red chiles
    2 cloves garlic, minced or pressed
    6 medium-size pear-shaped (Roma-type) tomatoes (about 12 oz. *total*), chopped
    ¾ cup dry white wine
    ¼ cup sliced pitted ripe olives
    1 tablespoon drained capers
    1½ teaspoons minced fresh oregano leaves or ½ teaspoon dry oregano leaves
    8 ounces dry gnocchi-shaped pasta
    1 pound tuna fillets or steaks, about ½ inch thick
       Salt and freshly ground pepper
    ¼ cup chopped Italian (flat-leaf) or curly-leaf parsley

Heat ¼ cup of the oil in a wide frying pan over medium heat. Add onion and chiles; cook, stirring often, until onion is soft (about 5 minutes). Stir in garlic, tomatoes, wine, olives, capers, and oregano. Adjust heat so mixture boils gently. Continue to cook, uncovered, stirring occasionally, until sauce is slightly thickened (10 to 15 minutes).

Meanwhile, in a 5- to 6-quart pan, cook pasta in 3 quarts boiling water just until tender to bite (10 to 12 minutes); or cook according to package directions. Drain well.

While pasta is cooking, rinse tuna, pat dry, and cut into serving-size pieces. Brush on all sides with remaining 1 tablespoon oil. Place a ridged cooktop grill pan over medium-high heat; heat until a drop of water dances on the surface. Place fish on hot pan and cook, turning once, until fish is just slightly translucent or wet inside; cut in thickest part to test (about 4 minutes *total*).

Season tomato sauce to taste with salt and pepper; stir in parsley. Slice tuna across the grain into bite-size strips. Place pasta in a warm serving bowl; top with sauce. Arrange tuna around edge. Makes 4 servings.

Per serving: 567 calories, 35 g protein, 50 g carbohydrates, 25 g total fat, 43 mg cholesterol, 175 mg sodium

Grilled Swordfish with Stir-fried Noodles

Preparation time: About 25 minutes

Marinating time: At least 30 minutes

Cooking time: About 20 minutes

Tender swordfish steaks are soaked in a flavorful soy marinade, then grilled and served on a bed of colorful, chile-seasoned Chinese noodles.

- ¼ **cup soy sauce**
- 2 **tablespoons seasoned rice vinegar (or 2 tablespoons rice or white wine vinegar mixed with ⅜ teaspoon sugar)**
- 1 **tablespoon Oriental sesame oil**
- 1 **to 1½ pounds swordfish steaks, ¾ to 1 inch thick**
- ¼ **cup salad oil**
- 2 **medium-size onions, thinly sliced**
- 3 **medium-size carrots (7 to 8 oz. *total*), coarsely shredded**
- 1 **medium-size red bell pepper (about 5 oz.), seeded and cut into thin bite-size strips**
- 1 **or 2 *each* small fresh hot red and green chiles, seeded and finely chopped**
- 3 **cloves garlic, minced or pressed**
- 1 **tablespoon grated fresh ginger**
- 1 **cup lightly packed fresh cilantro (coriander) leaves**
- 1 **package (14 oz.) fresh Chinese-style noodles**
- ½ **cup unsalted dry-roasted peanuts**

In a shallow baking dish, mix soy, vinegar, and sesame oil. Rinse swordfish, pat dry, and cut into serving-size pieces. Place fish in soy mixture and turn to coat well. Cover and refrigerate for at least 30 minutes or up to 1 hour.

Heat 2 tablespoons of the salad oil in a wide frying pan over medium heat. Add onions, carrots, bell pepper, and chiles. Cook, stirring often, until vegetables are tender-crisp to bite (about 5 minutes). Stir in garlic and ginger; cook for 30 more seconds. Add cilantro; cook and stir for a few seconds, just until cilantro turns bright green. Lift vegetable mixture from pan and set aside. Reserve pan.

In a 6- to 8-quart pan, cook noodles in 4 quarts boiling water just until barely tender to bite (2 to 3 minutes); or cook according to package directions. Drain well, rinse with hot water, and drain again.

Lift swordfish from baking dish, reserving marinade. Place an oiled ridged cooktop grill pan over medium heat; heat until a drop of water dances on the surface. Then place fish on hot pan and cook, turning once, until fish is just slightly translucent or

wet inside; cut in thickest part to test (7 to 10 minutes *total*).

Heat remaining 2 tablespoons salad oil in reserved frying pan over medium-high heat. Add noodles and peanuts. Cook, turning gently with 2 spoons, just until noodles are hot (1 to 2 minutes). Add stir-fried vegetables and reserved marinade. Cook, stirring gently, until heated through. Arrange noodle-vegetable mixture on a platter; arrange fish on top. Makes 4 to 6 servings.

Per serving: 628 calories, 38 g protein, 59 g carbohydrates, 28 g total fat, 138 mg cholesterol, 966 mg sodium

Fettuccine with Calamari

Preparation time: About 10 minutes

Cooking time: About 15 minutes

Cook the squid for this garlic-accented pasta main dish very briefly—just until the meat is opaque white. Overcooking can make the delicate shellfish unpleasantly tough.

- 1 **pound cleaned squid tubes (mantles) and tentacles**
- ⅓ **cup olive oil**
- 1 **large red onion, thinly sliced and separated into rings**
- 1 **package (9 oz.) fresh fettuccine or 8 ounces dry fettuccine**
- 3 **large cloves garlic, minced or pressed**
- 1 **tablespoon lemon juice**
- ¼ **cup finely chopped parsley**
  Salt and freshly ground pepper
  Lemon wedges

Cut squid tubes crosswise into ½-inch-wide strips; set squid strips and tentacles aside.

Heat oil in a wide frying pan over medium heat. Add onion and cook, stirring often, until very soft but not brown (8 to 10 minutes).

Meanwhile, in a 5- to 6-quart pan, cook fettuccine in 3 quarts boiling water until tender to bite (3 to 4 minutes for fresh pasta, 8 to 10 minutes for dry); or cook according to package directions. Drain well.

To onion, add garlic and squid strips and tentacles; cook, stirring constantly, just until squid is opaque (2 to 3 minutes). Mix in lemon juice. Add fettuccine and half the parsley; mix gently, using 2 spoons, until heated through. Season to taste with salt and pepper. Sprinkle with remaining parsley and garnish with lemon wedges. Makes 4 servings.

Per serving: 473 calories, 27 g protein, 44 g carbohydrates, 21 g total fat, 339 mg cholesterol, 71 mg sodium

Barbecued Crab with Spaghetti

Preparation time: About 20 minutes

Cooking time: About 55 minutes

Crab is at its messiest and most delicious here—it's served in a spicy barbecue sauce atop a platter of steaming spaghetti. You eat the crab legs and claws with your fingers, so be sure to provide plenty of big paper napkins.

- 2 tablespoons butter or margarine
- 1 large onion, finely chopped
- 3 cloves garlic, minced or pressed
- 1 can (14½ oz.) regular-strength chicken broth
- 1 can (8 oz.) tomato sauce
- 1 cup catsup
- ⅓ cup *each* white wine vinegar and firmly packed brown sugar
- 3 tablespoons Worcestershire
- 1 tablespoon soy sauce
- 1½ teaspoons dry mustard
- 1 teaspoon liquid hot pepper seasoning
- ½ teaspoon *each* celery seeds, ground allspice, and dry thyme leaves
- 2 dry bay leaves
- 2 large Dungeness crabs (3½ to 4 lbs. *total*), cooked, cleaned, and cracked
- 12 ounces to 1 pound dry spaghetti or spaghettini
  Chopped parsley

Melt butter in a 5- to 6-quart pan over medium-low heat. Add onion and garlic; cook, stirring often, until onion is soft but not brown (8 to 10 minutes). Stir in broth, tomato sauce, catsup, vinegar, sugar, Worcestershire, soy, mustard, hot pepper seasoning, celery seeds, allspice, thyme, and bay leaves. Increase heat to high and bring to a boil; reduce heat and boil very gently, uncovered, until reduced to 3 cups (about 45 minutes).

Meanwhile, remove body meat from crabs, discarding shells; set shelled body meat and cracked claws aside.

In a 6- to 8-quart pan, cook spaghetti in 4 quarts boiling water just until tender to bite (8 to 10 minutes); or cook according to package directions.

While spaghetti is cooking, add all the crab to sauce and simmer, uncovered, just until crab is heated through, stirring gently several times (about 5 minutes). Drain spaghetti well; transfer to a warm large serving bowl and top with crab sauce. Sprinkle with parsley. Makes 4 to 6 servings.

Per serving: 587 calories, 30 g protein, 98 g carbohydrates, 8 g total fat, 94 mg cholesterol, 1,821 mg sodium

---

Pictured on facing page

Seafood in Parchment

Preparation time: About 25 minutes

Cooking & baking time: About 30 minutes

Effortlessly elegant, this parchment-wrapped main dish showcases succulent shellfish in tomato sauce.

- 6 tablespoons olive oil
- 1 clove garlic, minced or pressed
- 1 can (15 oz.) tomato purée
- ½ cup dry white wine
- 2 tablespoons drained capers
- ½ cup finely chopped parsley
  Salt and pepper
- 8 ounces sea scallops, rinsed, drained, and cut crosswise into ½-inch-thick slices
- 12 medium-large raw shrimp (31 to 35 per lb.), shelled and deveined
- 12 small hard-shell clams in shells, suitable for steaming, scrubbed
- 12 mussels in shells, scrubbed, beards pulled off
- 6 ounces dry linguine

Heat 2 tablespoons of the oil in a 2- to 3-quart pan over medium-high heat. Add garlic and stir until soft (about 1 minute). Add tomato purée, wine, capers, and ¼ cup of the chopped parsley. Bring to a boil; then reduce heat and boil gently, uncovered, until sauce is slightly thickened (about 10 minutes). Season to taste with salt and pepper; set aside.

Cut 4 rectangles of cooking parchment, each 15 by 24 inches. Place scallops and shrimp in centers of rectangles; place clams and mussels alongside. Pour tomato sauce over scallops and shrimp.

To seal each packet, bring together short ends of parchment and fold over by 1 inch; then fold over by 1 inch a second time. Fold the open ends under 2 or 3 times; tuck under packet. Place packets in a single layer in a large, shallow rimmed baking pan.

Bake in a 425° oven until clams and mussels pop open (about 15 minutes). To check, open one end of one packet; if necessary, reseal and continue baking.

Meanwhile, in a 5- to 6-quart pan, cook linguine in 3 quarts boiling water just until tender to bite (8 to 10 minutes); or cook according to package directions. Drain well and place in a warm serving bowl. Mix in remaining ¼ cup oil and remaining ¼ cup chopped parsley; keep warm.

Transfer packets, seam sides up, to 4 dinner plates. At the table, open packets; fold back parchment and tuck under. Add linguine to each packet alongside seafood. Makes 4 servings.

Per serving: 518 calories, 32 g protein, 46 g carbohydrates, 24 g total fat, 152 mg cholesterol, 779 mg sodium

*Freshly cooked linguine completes each
serving of Seafood in Parchment (recipe on facing
page). Each fragrant little package holds oven-steamed
scallops, shrimp, clams, and mussels in a
tomato-wine sauce.*

51

Capellini

Angel Hair with Shrimp & Mint Butter Sauce

Preparation time: About 30 minutes

Cooking time: 12 to 15 minutes

Refreshingly minty, this combination of shrimp and very thin pasta is a fine dish for an elegant warm-weather dinner.

- 6 tablespoons butter or margarine
- ½ teaspoon grated lemon peel
- ½ cup lightly packed fresh mint leaves
- 1 pound medium-size raw shrimp (35 to 45 per lb.), shelled and deveined
- 8 ounces dry capellini or 1 package (9 oz.) fresh angel hair pasta
- 1 cup dry white wine
  Thin lemon wedges
  Fresh mint sprigs

In a food processor or blender, whirl ¼ cup of the butter, lemon peel, and the ½ cup mint leaves until well blended; set aside. If made ahead, cover and refrigerate for up to 1 day.

In a wide frying pan, melt remaining 2 tablespoons butter over medium heat. Add shrimp and cook, stirring, until opaque throughout; cut to test (3 to 4 minutes). Lift out shrimp and keep warm. Reserve drippings in pan.

In a 5- to 6-quart pan, cook capellini in 3 quarts boiling water just until tender to bite (about 3 minutes for dry pasta, 1 to 2 minutes for fresh); or cook according to package directions. Drain well.

While pasta is cooking, add wine to drippings in frying pan; bring to a boil over high heat. Boil, stirring, until reduced to ⅓ cup (about 5 minutes). Add mint butter (all in one chunk) and stir quickly until butter is completely blended into sauce. Stir in shrimp and remove from heat.

Divide pasta among 4 wide, shallow bowls. Spoon shrimp mixture over pasta. Garnish with lemon wedges and mint sprigs. Makes 4 servings.

Per serving: 463 calories, 26 g protein, 44 g carbohydrates, 20 g total fat, 186 mg cholesterol, 316 mg sodium

Tricolor Pasta with Brandied Shrimp

Preparation time: About 30 minutes

Cooking time: About 10 minutes

Thin strands of golden, spinach-green, and rosy tomato-flavored linguine mingle vividly with juicy shrimp flamed in a buttery sauce with sliced fresh mushrooms.

- 6 tablespoons butter or margarine
- 2 tablespoons lemon juice
- 1 pound medium-size raw shrimp (35 to 45 per lb.), shelled, deveined, and butterflied
- ¼ cup brandy
- ½ teaspoon *each* dry tarragon and Worcestershire
- ¼ teaspoon ground ginger
- 1 teaspoon Dijon mustard
- 6 ounces mushrooms, thinly sliced
  Salt
- 1 package (9 oz.) fresh tricolor linguine
  Chopped parsley

Melt 3 tablespoons of the butter in a wide frying pan over medium heat. Stir in lemon juice; cook, stirring, until bubbly. Add shrimp and cook, stirring often, until opaque throughout; cut to test (3 to 4 minutes). Meanwhile, heat brandy in a small pan over low heat until barely warm to the touch. Carefully pour brandy over shrimp; ignite at once. Stir gently until flames are gone. Lift out shrimp and set aside.

To drippings in pan, add remaining 3 tablespoons butter, tarragon, Worcestershire, ginger, and mustard. Stir until well combined. Increase heat to medium-high. Add mushrooms and cook, stirring often, until lightly browned (about 3 minutes). Return shrimp to pan and stir lightly just until heated through (about 1 minute). Season to taste with salt.

Meanwhile, in a 5- to 6-quart pan, cook linguine in 3 quarts boiling water just until tender to bite (about 4 minutes); or cook according to package directions. Drain well.

Divide pasta among 4 heated dinner plates, then spoon shrimp sauce over pasta. Garnish with parsley. Makes 4 servings.

Per serving: 450 calories, 28 g protein, 39 g carbohydrates, 21 g total fat, 261 mg cholesterol, 377 mg sodium

Scallops & Green Noodles

Preparation time: About 25 minutes

Cooking time: 12 to 15 minutes

Barely cooked slivers of carrot, bell pepper, and green onion add color and crisp texture to this creamy blend of spinach noodles and scallops.

- 2 **large carrots (6 to 8 oz. *total*)**
- 1 **large red bell pepper (about 8 oz.), quartered and seeded**
- 8 **green onions (including tops)**
- 1 **pound sea scallops, rinsed and drained**
- ½ **cup (¼ lb.) butter or margarine**
- ⅔ **cup dry white wine**
- 1½ **cups whipping cream**
- 1 **package (9 oz.) fresh green fettuccine or 8 ounces dry green fettuccine**
  Salt and pepper
  Freshly grated nutmeg

Cut carrots, bell pepper, and onions into slivers ⅛ inch thick and 2 to 3 inches long. Set aside in separate piles. Cut scallops into ¼-inch-thick slices; set aside.

Melt 2 tablespoons of the butter in a wide frying pan over high heat. Add carrots and cook, stirring, until slightly limp (about 1 minute); lift out and set aside. Add 1 tablespoon more butter and bell pepper; cook, stirring, until slightly limp (about 1 minute). Lift out and add to carrots. Add onions and 1 tablespoon more butter; stir just until hot (30 to 45 seconds). Add to carrots and pepper; set aside.

Add wine to pan and bring to a boil. Add scallops, reduce heat, cover, and simmer until scallops are opaque throughout; cut to test (2 to 3 minutes). Lift scallops from pan with a slotted spoon and add to vegetables; keep warm.

Add cream to liquid in pan, increase heat to high, and bring to a full boil. Boil, uncovered, until reduced to 1¾ cups. Reduce heat to low, then add remaining ¼ cup butter and stir until smoothly blended into sauce.

While you are finishing sauce, in a 5- to 6-quart pan, cook fettuccine in 3 quarts boiling water just until tender to bite (3 to 4 minutes for fresh pasta, 5 to 7 minutes for dry); or cook according to package directions. Drain well. Add pasta to hot cream sauce; mix lightly, using 2 forks. Add scallops and vegetables and mix gently. Season to taste with salt, pepper, and nutmeg. Makes 4 to 6 servings.

Per serving: 642 calories, 26 g protein, 39 g carbohydrates, 44 g total fat, 220 mg cholesterol, 421 mg sodium

Ginger Linguine with Smoked Scallops

Preparation time: About 5 minutes

Smoking time: 12 to 15 minutes

Cooking time: 10 to 12 minutes

The woodsy flavor of oven-smoked scallops blends hauntingly with fresh ginger and cream in this rich sauce for linguine.

- 1 **pound scallops, rinsed and patted dry**
- 3 **tablespoons liquid smoke**
- 8 **ounces dry linguine or 1 package (9 oz.) fresh linguine**
- 1½ **tablespoons *each* tarragon wine vinegar and grated fresh ginger**
- ¼ **cup thinly sliced shallots**
- 1 **cup whipping cream**
- ½ **cup dry white wine**
- 1 **teaspoon Dijon mustard**
  Chopped parsley

If scallops are large, cut them into bite-size pieces. Pour liquid smoke into a 5- to 6-quart pan with ovenproof handles. Set a perforated or wire rack in pan. Arrange scallops in a single layer on rack and cover tightly. Bake in a 350° oven until scallops are opaque throughout; cut to test (12 to 15 minutes). If made ahead, let scallops cool; then cover and refrigerate for up to 1 day.

While scallops are smoking, in another 5- to 6-quart pan, cook linguine in 3 quarts boiling water just until tender to bite (8 to 10 minutes for dry pasta, 1 to 2 minutes for fresh); or cook according to package directions. Drain well.

While pasta is cooking, combine vinegar, ginger, and shallots in a wide frying pan over high heat; cook until vinegar has evaporated (about 1 minute). Add cream, wine, and mustard. Bring to a full boil; then boil, uncovered, stirring often, until sauce is reduced to 1¼ cups. Reduce heat to medium; add scallops and mix lightly until heated through (1 to 2 minutes). Add linguine; mix lightly, using 2 spoons. Sprinkle with parsley. Makes 4 servings.

Per serving: 496 calories, 28 g protein, 50 g carbohydrates, 20 g total fat, 104 mg cholesterol, 245 mg sodium

Bake pasta corkscrews beneath a fluffy
blanket of cream cheese and butter, then top them with
golden chicken legs to make this family-style feast:
Tomato-Cheese Pasta with Baked Chicken
(recipe on facing page).

Poultry

Chicken and noodles—to single out one well-known combination—illustrate the enduring popularity of pasta and poultry. Whether you choose familiar fettuccine or fanciful cockscombs, whether the meat is chicken, turkey, or something a bit more exotic, the finished dish is bound to be a hit.

And though the typical recipe calls for pasta as a foundation and poultry as the crowning touch, it's perfectly possible to vary the scheme. In Orzo-stuffed Roast Chicken & Vegetables, for example, tiny rice-shaped pasta is hidden within the cavity of a roast chicken. In Mexican Chicken Lasagne, the poultry is layered between the pasta ribbons; and in Won Ton Ravioli, ground chicken fills plump little pasta pillows.

Pictured on facing page

Tomato-Cheese Pasta with Baked Chicken

Preparation time: About 10 minutes

Cooking time: 8 to 10 minutes

Baking time: About 45 minutes

Bake chicken legs until they're almost done, then open the oven and slip in the pasta—a casserole of spiral-shaped *cavatappi* blanketed with snowy whipped cheese and dotted with diced tomatoes.

> 4 to 6 whole chicken legs, thighs attached (2 to 3 lbs. *total*)
>
> 8 ounces dry corkscrew-shaped pasta (cavatappi)
>
> 1 tablespoon olive oil
>
> 1 large package (8 oz.) Neufchâtel or cream cheese, at room temperature
>
> ½ cup (¼ lb.) unsalted butter or margarine, at room temperature
>
> ⅓ cup grated Parmesan cheese
>
> 3 medium-size pear-shaped (Roma-type) tomatoes (about 6 oz. *total*), chopped
>
> 1 tablespoon chopped fresh basil or 1 teaspoon dry basil
>
> Fresh basil sprigs

Rinse chicken legs, pat dry, and place, skin sides up, in a single layer in a shallow rimmed baking pan. Bake, uncovered, in a 400° oven for 35 minutes.

Meanwhile, in a 5- to 6-quart pan, cook pasta in 3 quarts boiling water just until tender to bite (8 to 10 minutes); or cook according to package directions. Drain; place in a shallow 2- to 3-quart baking dish, lightly mix in oil, and set aside.

In a medium-size bowl, combine Neufchâtel cheese, butter, and ¼ cup of the Parmesan cheese; beat with an electric mixer until well blended. Mound cheese mixture over center of pasta; sprinkle tomatoes over cheese mixture.

When chicken has baked for 35 minutes, place cheese-topped pasta in oven. Bake, uncovered, until pasta is hot in center and meat near chicken thighbone is no longer pink; cut to test (about 10 minutes). If desired, arrange chicken over pasta around edge of baking dish. Sprinkle with chopped basil and remaining Parmesan cheese; garnish with basil sprigs. Makes 4 to 6 servings.

Per serving: 763 calories, 42 g protein, 37 g carbohydrates, 49 g total fat, 191 mg cholesterol, 383 mg sodium

Orzo-stuffed Roast Chicken & Vegetables

Preparation time: About 45 minutes

Cooking time: About 15 minutes

Roasting time: 1 to 1¼ hours

Tiny rice-shaped pasta cooked in chicken broth with fresh chard and flavorful dried mushrooms makes a tempting dressing for a plump whole chicken. You'll find the pasta sold under several names, among them *orzo* and *riso*.

Creste di Galli

Orzo & Chard Stuffing (recipe follows)
1 **large frying chicken (3½ to 4 lbs.)**
2 **medium-size onions, unpeeled, cut lengthwise into quarters**
4 **large carrots (about 1 lb.** *total***), cut lengthwise into quarters**
¼ **cup olive oil**
1 **tablespoon lemon juice**
2 **cloves garlic, minced or pressed**
1 **teaspoon dry rosemary, crumbled**
Lemon wedges

Prepare Orzo & Chard Stuffing; set aside to cool slightly.

Remove chicken neck and giblets; reserve for other uses, if desired. Remove and discard lumps of fat from chicken cavity. Rinse chicken inside and out; pat dry. Fill cavity with stuffing; close cavity with skewers. Spoon remaining stuffing into a greased 2- to 3-cup casserole, cover, and set aside.

Place chicken, breast up, in a shallow roasting pan. Surround with onions and carrots. Mix oil, lemon juice, garlic, and rosemary; brush some of the mixture generously over chicken, then drizzle remainder over vegetables. Roast, uncovered, in a 375° oven until a meat thermometer inserted in thickest part of chicken thigh (not touching bone) registers 185°F or until meat near thighbone is no longer pink; cut to test (1 to 1¼ hours). Vegetables should be tender when pierced. Bake stuffing in casserole for last 10 to 15 minutes.

Transfer chicken and vegetables to a serving platter. Garnish with lemon wedges. To serve, spoon out stuffing and carve chicken. Serve chicken and stuffing with vegetables. Makes 4 to 6 servings.

Orzo & Chard Stuffing. In a medium-size bowl, soak ½ cup (about ½ oz.) **dried mushrooms** in **hot water** to cover until soft (20 to 30 minutes). Drain well; cut off and discard any hard stems. Set mushrooms aside. Coarsely chop 4 **Swiss chard leaves** (about 3 oz. *total*) to make about 2 cups, lightly packed; set aside.

Heat 2 tablespoons **olive oil** in a 2-quart pan over medium heat. Add 1 small **onion,** finely chopped; cook, stirring often, until soft but not brown (about 5 minutes). Stir in mushrooms and 1 cup (about 8 oz.) **dry rice-shaped pasta.** Add 1 can (14½ oz.) **regular-strength chicken broth.** Bring to a boil; reduce heat and boil gently, uncovered, stirring occasionally, until broth is absorbed but pasta is still slightly chewy (8 to 10 minutes). Stir in chard. Season to taste with **salt** and **pepper.** Cover and let stand until slightly cooled (about 15 minutes).

Per serving: 744 calories, 49 g protein, 49 g carbohydrates, 38 g total fat, 132 mg cholesterol, 555 mg sodium

Rooster Crests with Mustard Chicken

Preparation time: 5 minutes

Cooking time: About 55 minutes

This isn't exactly a traditional American dish, but you'll still be reminded of your grandmother's Sunday stewed chicken and noodles! Whole chicken legs are simmered in a creamy sauce enlivened with a sophisticated mustard, then served atop whimsically shaped pasta cockscombs (*creste di galli*). Serve with Sunday-dinner favorites—fresh peas and hot, buttery biscuits with honey.

 6 whole chicken legs, thighs attached (2½ to 3 lbs. *total*)
 2 cups water
 2 chicken bouillon cubes
 ¼ cup butter or margarine
 ¼ cup all-purpose flour
 1 cup milk or half-and-half
 2 tablespoons Dijon mustard
 ½ teaspoon dry thyme leaves
   Salt and pepper
 1 package (12 oz.) dry rooster-crest pasta
 ¼ cup finely chopped parsley

Rinse chicken and pat dry; then place in a wide, heavy 4- to 5-quart pan with water and bouillon cubes. Bring to a boil over medium-high heat, stirring as needed to dissolve bouillon cubes. Reduce heat, cover, and simmer for 30 minutes. Lift out chicken and set aside. Skim and discard fat from broth, then measure out 1¾ cups broth. Reserve remaining broth for other uses.

In pan used to cook chicken, melt butter over medium heat. Blend in flour and cook, stirring constantly, until bubbly. Remove from heat; gradually stir in the 1¾ cups broth, then milk, until blended. Return to heat and continue to cook, stirring, until mixture boils and thickens. Blend in mustard and thyme; season to taste with salt and pepper.

Remove and discard skin from chicken. Place chicken in sauce and simmer, uncovered, until chicken is tender and meat near thighbone is no longer pink; cut to test (about 15 minutes).

Meanwhile, in a 6- to 8-quart pan, cook pasta in 4 quarts boiling water just until tender to bite (8 to 10 minutes); or cook according to package directions. Drain well and mound in center of a warm deep platter.

Lift chicken from sauce and arrange around edge of platter. Stir parsley into sauce; pour sauce over pasta and chicken. Makes 6 servings.

Per serving: 472 calories, 33 g protein, 50 g carbohydrates, 15 g total fat, 121 mg cholesterol, 672 mg sodium

Spaghetti with Chicken Chili Sauce

Preparation time: About 30 minutes

Cooking time: About 1 hour

The distinctive aroma is reminiscent of *chili con carne*—but here, traditional chili seasonings go into a pungent sauce for spaghetti and gently poached, shredded chicken.

 1 frying chicken (3 to 3½ lbs.), quartered
 2 tablespoons butter or margarine
 1 large onion, finely chopped
 2 cloves garlic, minced or pressed
2½ teaspoons chili powder
 2 teaspoons ground cumin
 3 cans (15 oz. *each*) tomato purée
 1 pound dry spaghetti
 2 cups (8 oz.) shredded jack cheese

Rinse chicken and pat dry. Place in a deep 5- to 6-quart pan and add enough water to barely cover. Bring to a boil over medium-high heat. Reduce heat, cover, and simmer until meat near thighbone is no longer pink; cut to test (about 30 minutes). Lift out chicken and let cool slightly; reserve broth for other uses. Remove and discard chicken skin and bones; tear meat into bite-size pieces and set aside.

Melt butter in a wide frying pan over medium heat. Add onion and cook, stirring often, until soft but not brown (about 5 minutes). Mix in garlic, chili powder, cumin, and tomato purée. Reduce heat and simmer, uncovered, for 15 minutes.

Meanwhile, in a 6- to 8-quart pan, cook spaghetti in 4 quarts boiling water just until tender to bite (10 to 12 minutes); or cook according to package directions. Drain well and place in a warm large serving bowl.

About 5 minutes before spaghetti is done, add chicken to sauce and simmer just until hot. Spoon sauce over spaghetti; serve with cheese to add to taste. Makes 6 servings.

Per serving: 719 calories, 48 g protein, 80 g carbohydrates, 23 g total fat, 122 mg cholesterol, 1,113 mg sodium

Chicken & Noodles with Pimentos

Preparation time: About 25 minutes

Roasting time: About 1¼ hours

Cooking time: About 10 minutes

The familiar combination of chicken and noodles sheds its homey, everyday image here! Fettuccine and roast chicken mingle with cream and colorful fresh pimento, orange zest, and cilantro.

 1 large frying chicken (3½ to 4 lbs.)
 1 large orange (about 8 oz.)
 2 large fresh pimentos or red bell peppers (about 12 oz. *total*), seeded and cut into thin strips
 2 cups whipping cream
 1 teaspoon crushed dried hot red chiles
   Salt and pepper
 1 package (9 or 10 oz.) fresh fettuccine or tagliarini
 ½ cup fresh cilantro (coriander) leaves

Remove chicken neck and giblets; reserve for other uses, if desired. Remove and discard lumps of fat from chicken cavity. Rinse chicken inside and out; pat dry. Place chicken, breast up, in a shallow roasting pan. Roast, uncovered, in a 400° oven until a meat thermometer inserted in thickest part of thigh (not touching bone) registers 185°F or until meat near thighbone is no longer pink; cut to test (about 1 hour). Drain juices from chicken into roasting pan; set chicken aside. Scrape drippings, including browned bits, from pan and reserve.

When chicken is cool enough to handle, pull off skin in large pieces; place, fat side down, on a rack in roasting pan. Return to 400° oven and bake, uncovered, until very crisp (15 to 20 minutes).

Meanwhile, remove and discard chicken bones; tear meat into bite-size pieces and set aside. With a zester, remove peel (colored part only) from orange. (Or use a vegetable peeler, then cut peel into fine strands with a knife.) Reserve orange for other uses.

Combine pan drippings and pimentos in a wide frying pan; cook over medium-high heat, stirring often, until pimentos are slightly softened (3 to 5 minutes). Add cream, chiles, and half the orange peel. Increase heat to high and boil until reduced by half (about 5 minutes). Add chicken meat and cook just until hot; season to taste with salt and pepper.

Meanwhile, in a 5- to 6-quart pan, cook fettuccine in 3 quarts boiling water just until tender to bite (3 to 4 minutes); or cook according to package directions. Drain well. Add pasta to chicken mixture, remove from heat, and mix lightly, using 2 forks. Transfer to a warm deep platter. Crumble chicken skin over pasta; garnish with cilantro and remaining orange peel. Makes about 6 servings.

Per serving: 731 calories, 38 g protein, 30 g carbohydrates, 51 g total fat, 265 mg cholesterol, 157 mg sodium

Pictured on facing page

Oven Chicken & Linguine

Preparation time: About 10 minutes

Baking time: About 45 minutes

Cooking time: About 10 minutes

For this one-dish meal, bake chicken thighs until golden, then toss linguine and spinach with the pan drippings.

 ½ cup (¼ lb.) butter or margarine
 1 medium-size onion, thinly sliced
 2 cloves garlic, minced or pressed
 1 tablespoon dry basil
 ½ teaspoon crushed dried hot red chiles
 8 chicken thighs (about 2½ lbs. *total*)
 2 packages (10 oz. *each*) frozen chopped spinach, thawed
 8 ounces dry linguine
 1 cup (about 5 oz.) grated Parmesan cheese
   Salt
 1 small orange (about 6 oz.), cut into wedges
   Fresh basil sprigs

Melt butter in a 10- by 15-inch shallow rimmed baking pan in a 400° oven. Remove pan from oven; stir onion, garlic, dry basil, and chiles into butter. Rinse chicken and pat dry; then place, skin side down, in butter mixture and turn to coat. Bake, uncovered, until meat near bone is no longer pink; cut to test (about 45 minutes). Meanwhile, squeeze as much liquid as possible from spinach.

Ten minutes before chicken is done, in a 5- to 6-quart pan, cook linguine in 3 quarts boiling water just until tender to bite (8 to 10 minutes); or cook according to package directions. Drain well.

Lift chicken from baking pan and keep warm. Add spinach to pan and stir over medium heat to scrape up browned bits. Remove from heat. Add linguine and cheese; mix lightly, using 2 forks. Season to taste with salt.

Mound linguine mixture on dinner plates; arrange chicken alongside. Garnish with orange wedges and basil sprigs. Makes 4 to 6 servings.

Per serving: 866 calories, 51 g protein, 40 g carbohydrates, 56 g total fat, 263 mg cholesterol, 865 mg sodium

For an appealing one-dish meal, try these tender chicken thighs accompanied by chile-dotted pasta with spinach and cheese. A squeeze of orange adds the finishing touch to Oven Chicken & Linguine (recipe on facing page).

Purchased won ton, egg roll (spring roll), and pot sticker (*gyoza*) wrappers can help you turn out Italian ravioli, cannelloni, and tortellini at record speed. You omit the time-consuming step of making, rolling, and cutting fresh pasta dough, yet the results are still impressive and delicious. In fact, you might even prefer ready-made to homemade wrappers, since some purchased varieties are thinner than homemade pasta. The thinness also makes them fragile, though—so handle them gently when cooking and saucing.

Because these Asian wrappers are generous in size, they hold more filling than their classic counterparts, making rather large versions of each pasta specialty.

Won ton and other wrappers are sold in the produce section of most supermarkets; you'll also find them in Asian markets.

Shiitake & Cheese Cannelloni

2 ounces (2½ to 3 cups) dried shiitake mushrooms
1½ pounds button mushrooms, thinly sliced
7 tablespoons butter or margarine
1 clove garlic, minced or pressed
3 tablespoons white wine vinegar
1½ tablespoons soy sauce
⅔ cup dry sherry
1½ tablespoons minced fresh ginger
1¼ teaspoons dry mustard
1¾ teaspoons ground coriander
¼ cup all-purpose flour
1½ cups regular-strength chicken broth
¾ cup milk
3 cups (12 oz.) shredded Münster cheese
8 egg roll wrappers, *each* about 6 inches square

Won Ton Ravioli & More

In a medium-size bowl, soak shiitake mushrooms in warm water to cover until soft and pliable (20 to 30 minutes). Drain and rinse well. Cut off and discard stems; set aside 8 small caps for garnish. Thinly slice remaining caps and add to sliced button mushrooms.

Melt ¼ cup of the butter in a 5- to 6-quart pan over medium-high heat. Add sliced mushrooms and garlic; cook, stirring often, until liquid has evaporated and mushrooms are browned (about 25 minutes). Add vinegar, soy, ⅓ cup of the sherry, 1 tablespoon of the ginger, ¾ teaspoon of the mustard, and 1 teaspoon of the coriander. Cook, stirring, until liquid has evaporated (about 5 minutes); set aside.

Melt remaining 3 tablespoons butter in a 3- to 4-quart pan over medium-high heat. Blend in flour, remaining 1½ teaspoons ginger, remaining ½ teaspoon mustard, and remaining ¾ teaspoon coriander. Cook, stirring constantly, until bubbly. Remove from heat and gradually stir in broth and milk. Return to heat and continue to cook, stirring, until sauce comes to a rapid boil (about 3 minutes). Remove from heat and add 2 cups of the cheese and remaining ⅓ cup sherry; stir until cheese is melted. Mix 1 cup of the sauce into mushrooms.

Place egg roll wrappers on a flat surface. Spoon an eighth of the mushroom mixture along one end of each, then roll up wrapper from that end to enclose filling.

Spread ½ cup of the sauce in a 9- by 13-inch baking dish; place cannelloni in sauce, side by side and seam side down. Spoon remaining sauce evenly over cannelloni to cover;

sprinkle with remaining 1 cup cheese. Garnish with reserved shiitake caps. (At this point, you may cover and refrigerate for up to 1 day.)

Bake, uncovered, in a 425° oven until cannelloni are hot in center and sauce is bubbly (10 to 20 minutes). Makes 4 servings.

Per serving: 790 calories, 34 g protein, 57 g carbohydrates, 50 g total fat, 189 mg cholesterol, 1,548 mg sodium

Won Ton Ravioli

Chicken & Prosciutto Filling (facing page)
About 6 dozen won ton wrappers (about 1 lb. *total*)
1 egg white, beaten just to blend
Mushroom-Tomato Sauce (facing page)
¾ to 1 cup grated Parmesan cheese

Prepare Chicken & Prosciutto Filling. Place a won ton wrapper on a flat surface (cover remaining wrappers with plastic wrap to prevent drying). Place 1 rounded tablespoon filling on wrapper; spread evenly to within about ⅜ inch of edges. Brush edges with egg white. Cover with another wrapper and press edges well to seal. If desired, use a pastry wheel to trim edges decoratively; discard trimmings.

Repeat to make more ravioli, using remaining filling; as ravioli are completed, place in a single layer in flour-dusted shallow baking pans and cover with plastic wrap. (At this point, you may cover and refrigerate for up to 4 hours. Or freeze ravioli in baking pans until firm, then transfer to containers and store in freezer for up to 1 month.)

Prepare Mushroom-Tomato Sauce. When sauce is almost done, in a 6- to 8-quart pan, cook ravioli, about half at a time, in 4 quarts gently boiling water just until they are tender to bite (about 5 minutes if fresh, 6 minutes if frozen). Lift ravioli from water with a slotted spoon and place on warm plates or a deep platter; spoon Mushroom-Tomato Sauce over each layer of ravioli. Serve with cheese to add to taste. Makes 6 servings (about 3 dozen ravioli).

Chicken & Prosciutto Filling.

Coarsely chop 6 ounces thinly sliced **prosciutto** or ham. Remove and discard bones and skin from 1 pound **chicken breasts;** cut meat into ½-inch pieces. Melt 2 tablespoons **butter** or margarine in a wide frying pan over medium heat. Add 1 large **onion,** chopped; cook, stirring often, until onion is soft (6 to 8 minutes). Add chicken and cook, stirring, until it loses its pink color (about 3 minutes). Mix in prosciutto, then whirl the mixture in a food processor until coarsely ground (or chop finely with a knife). Mix in 2 **egg yolks,** ⅔ cup grated **Parmesan cheese,** 8 ounces **ricotta cheese,** and ⅛ to ¼ teaspoon **ground nutmeg;** season to taste with **salt** and **ground white pepper.** If made ahead, cover and refrigerate for up to 8 hours.

Mushroom-Tomato Sauce.

Melt 3 tablespoons **butter** or margarine in a wide frying pan over medium heat. Stir in ½ cup chopped **shallots** or onion and 1 pound **mushrooms,** thinly sliced. Cook, stirring often, until mushrooms are lightly browned. Stir in 2 tablespoons **tomato paste,** 1 teaspoon **dry basil,** and 2 cups *each* **dry vermouth** and **regular-strength chicken broth.** Increase heat to high and bring to a boil. Cook, stirring often, until reduced to 3 cups. Reduce heat to low. (At this point, you may let cool, then cover and refrigerate for up to 1 day. Reheat before continuing.)

Add 1 cup (½ lb.) **butter** or margarine to sauce; stir constantly until

butter is smoothly blended into sauce (butter thickens sauce). Serve at once.

Per serving: 903 calories, 48 g protein, 63 g carbohydrates, 52 g total fat, 333 mg cholesterol, 1,670 mg sodium

Pot Sticker Tortellini

Sausage-Spinach Filling (recipe follows)
6 to 7 dozen thin pot sticker (*gyoza*) or won ton wrappers (about 1 lb. *total*)
1 egg white, beaten just to blend
Cream Sauce (recipe follows)
2 tablespoons butter or margarine
1¾ to 2 cups (9 to 10 oz.) grated Parmesan cheese
Freshly grated nutmeg

Prepare Sausage-Spinach Filling.

Fill wrappers a few at a time. (If using won ton wrappers, use a 3- to 3¼-inch round cookie cutter to cut several wrappers at a time; discard trimmings.) Cover remaining wrappers with plastic wrap to prevent drying.

To shape tortellini, place about 1 teaspoon of the filling in center of a wrapper; moisten edge of wrapper with egg white, fold wrapper in half, and press edges together to seal. Bring ends together to overlap; moisten with egg white and press to seal. Repeat to make more tortellini, using remaining filling; as tortellini are

completed, place in a single layer in flour-dusted shallow baking pans and cover with plastic wrap. (At this point, you may cover and refrigerate for up to 4 hours. Or freeze tortellini in baking pans until firm, then transfer to containers and store in freezer for up to 1 month.)

Prepare Cream Sauce.

In a 6- to 8-quart pan, cook tortellini, half at a time, in 4 quarts gently boiling water just until tender to bite (about 4 minutes if fresh, 6 minutes if frozen). Lift tortellini from water with a slotted spoon and add to Cream Sauce along with butter and 1 cup of the cheese. Turn tortellini gently in sauce until coated. Sprinkle with nutmeg; serve with remaining ¾ to 1 cup cheese to add to taste. Makes 6 servings.

Sausage-Spinach Filling.

Remove and discard casings from 6 ounces **mild Italian sausages.** Crumble meat into a wide frying pan over medium-low heat. Cook, stirring often, until lightly browned. Remove from heat; spoon off and discard drippings. Squeeze as much liquid as possible from 1 package (10 oz.) thawed **frozen chopped spinach.** Combine sausage, spinach, 8 ounces **ricotta cheese,** 1 **egg yolk,** ½ cup grated **Parmesan cheese,** ⅛ teaspoon **pepper,** and ¾ teaspoon *each* crushed **fennel seeds** and **dry oregano leaves.** If made ahead, cover and refrigerate for up to 8 hours.

Cream Sauce.

In a wide frying pan, combine 3 cups **whipping cream** and ⅛ teaspoon **ground nutmeg.** Bring to a boil over high heat, then boil until large shiny bubbles form all over and sauce is reduced by about a third. Keep warm over lowest heat, stirring occasionally.

Per serving: 891 calories, 36 g protein, 51 g carbohydrates, 61 g total fat, 320 mg cholesterol, 973 mg sodium

*Dried tomatoes add a toasty-sweet accent to
Chicken in Port Cream with Fettuccine (recipe on facing
page). Steamed fresh asparagus is a good accompaniment
for this elegant entrée.*

Pasta & Chicken with Sweet-Sour Tomato Sauce

Preparation time: About 15 minutes

Cooking & grilling time: About 20 minutes

Distinctively seasoned with allspice, currants, and pine nuts, this fresh tomato sauce is delightful with tender linguine and strips of grilled chicken.

- 5 **tablespoons olive oil**
- 1 **medium-size onion, thinly sliced**
- 2 **tablespoons pine nuts or slivered almonds**
- 2 **cloves garlic, minced or pressed**
- 6 **medium-size pear-shaped (Roma-type) tomatoes (about 12 oz. *total*), chopped**
- 1 **tablespoon *each* firmly packed brown sugar and dried currants**
- 2 **tablespoons cider vinegar**
- ½ **teaspoon ground allspice**
- ¾ **cup dry red wine**
- 2 **whole chicken breasts (about 1 lb. *each*), skinned, boned, and split**
- 8 **ounces dry linguine or 1 package (9 oz.) fresh linguine**
  Salt and pepper
  Chopped parsley

Heat ¼ cup of the oil in a wide frying pan over medium heat. Add onion and pine nuts and cook, stirring, until onion is soft (about 5 minutes). Stir in garlic, tomatoes, sugar, currants, vinegar, allspice, and wine. Adjust heat so mixture boils gently. Continue to cook, uncovered, stirring occasionally, until sauce is slightly thickened (12 to 15 minutes).

Meanwhile, rinse chicken and pat dry. Brush on all sides with remaining 1 tablespoon oil. Place a ridged cooktop grill pan over medium heat; heat until a drop of water dances on the surface. Place chicken on hot pan and cook, turning once, until well browned on outside and no longer pink in center; cut chicken in thickest part to test (about 10 minutes *total*).

While chicken is cooking, in a 5- to 6-quart pan, cook linguine in 3 quarts boiling water just until tender to bite (8 to 10 minutes for dry pasta, 1 to 2 minutes for fresh); or cook according to package directions. Drain well.

Season tomato sauce to taste with salt and pepper. Add linguine and mix lightly, using 2 forks. Transfer to a warm deep platter. Cut chicken into ½-inch-wide strips; arrange around edge of linguine. Sprinkle with parsley. Makes 4 servings.

Per serving: 592 calories, 43 g protein, 55 g carbohydrates, 22 g total fat, 86 mg cholesterol, 108 mg sodium

---

Pictured on facing page

Chicken in Port Cream with Fettuccine

Soaking time: About 1 hour

Preparation time: 3 to 5 minutes

Cooking time: About 30 minutes

An unusual combination of ingredients produces decidedly elegant results in this simple-to-make dish. Be sure to use *dry* dried tomatoes, not the kind packed in olive oil.

- ¾ **cup dried tomatoes**
- 3 **whole chicken breasts (about 1 lb. *each*), skinned, boned, and split**
- 3 **tablespoons butter or margarine**
- 1 **cup port**
- 1½ **cups whipping cream**
- 1 **package (9 oz.) fresh fettuccine or 8 ounces dry fettuccine**
  Salt and pepper
  Fresh tarragon sprigs

In a small bowl, soak tomatoes in warm water to cover until soft (about 1 hour). Drain well, chop coarsely, and set aside.

Rinse chicken; pat dry. Melt butter in a wide frying pan over medium-high heat. Add chicken and cook, turning once, until well browned on outside and no longer pink in center; cut in thickest part to test (about 10 minutes *total*). Lift out chicken and keep warm.

To pan drippings, add port and cream. Increase heat to high and bring to a boil; boil, uncovered, stirring occasionally, until large, shiny bubbles form (10 to 15 minutes). Meanwhile, in a 5- to 6-quart pan, cook fettuccine in 3 quarts boiling water just until tender to bite (3 to 4 minutes for fresh pasta, 8 to 10 minutes for dry); or cook according to package directions.

While pasta is cooking, mix tomatoes, chicken, and any chicken juices into cream mixture; season to taste with salt and pepper.

Drain fettuccine well; transfer to a warm deep platter. Top with chicken mixture, then garnish with tarragon sprigs. Makes 6 servings.

Per serving: 541 calories, 41 g protein, 32 g carbohydrates, 27 g total fat, 217 mg cholesterol, 195 mg sodium

Farfalle with Grilled Chicken & Pesto Cream

Pictured on front cover

Preparation time: About 15 minutes

Cooking time: 15 to 20 minutes

How would you describe the shape of the pasta in this creamy green combination? The Italians see these little noodles as butterflies or *farfalle*; to others, they may look more like bow ties.

- 2 tablespoons pine nuts
  Minted Pesto Butter (recipe follows)
- 2 whole chicken breasts (about 1 lb. *each*), skinned, boned, and split
- 1 tablespoon olive oil
- 10 ounces dry bow-shaped pasta
- ¼ cup dry white wine
- 1 cup whipping cream
  Salt
- 2 tablespoons chopped roasted red pepper
  Fresh basil sprigs
- ⅓ to ½ cup grated Parmesan cheese

Stir pine nuts in a small frying pan over medium-low heat until lightly browned (about 3 minutes). Prepare Minted Pesto Butter, using 1 tablespoon of the pine nuts; set Minted Pesto Butter and remaining 1 tablespoon pine nuts aside.

Rinse chicken and pat dry. Brush on all sides with oil. Place a ridged cooktop grill pan over medium heat; heat until a drop of water dances on the surface. Place chicken on hot pan and cook, turning once, until well browned on outside and no longer pink in center; cut in thickest part to test (about 10 minutes *total*). Cut chicken into ½-inch-wide bite-size strips.

While chicken is cooking, in a 5- to 6-quart pan, cook pasta in 3 quarts boiling water just until tender to bite (about 10 minutes); or cook according to package directions. Drain well and set aside.

In a wide frying pan, combine Minted Pesto Butter and wine. Cook over medium heat, stirring occasionally, until bubbly (about 2 minutes). Stir in cream and bring to a full rolling boil, stirring often. Season sauce to taste with salt, then add roasted pepper, pasta, and chicken; mix lightly, using 2 spoons. Sprinkle mixture with remaining 1 tablespoon toasted pine nuts and garnish with basil sprigs. Serve with Parmesan cheese to add to taste. Makes 4 to 6 servings.

Minted Pesto Butter. In a blender or food processor, combine 1 tablespoon of the **toasted pine nuts;** 1 clove **garlic,** coarsely chopped; ½ cup *each* lightly packed **parsley sprigs** and **fresh basil leaves;** 2 tablespoons coarsely chopped **fresh mint leaves;** 1 **green onion** (including top), sliced; ⅛ teaspoon **pepper;** a pinch of **ground nutmeg;** 2 tablespoons **olive oil;** and ¼ cup **butter** or margarine, melted. Whirl until well combined, scraping sides of container several times.

Per serving: 711 calories, 40 g protein, 45 g carbohydrates, 41 g total fat, 205 mg cholesterol, 319 mg sodium

Fettuccine Verde with Chicken

Preparation time: About 25 minutes

Cooking time: About 20 minutes

Give leftover chicken a delicious encore with this colorful pasta dish. It's good with warm garlic bread and a ruffly green salad in a tart vinaigrette.

- 3 tablespoons olive oil
- 1 large onion, thinly sliced
- 8 ounces mushrooms, thinly sliced
- 2 cloves garlic, minced or pressed
- ¼ cup butter or margarine
- 1 package (3 oz.) thinly sliced ham, cut into julienne strips
- 1 medium-size tomato (about 5 oz.), chopped
- 1 teaspoon dry basil
- 1 package (9 oz.) fresh green fettuccine or 8 ounces dry green fettuccine
- 2 cups shredded cooked chicken
- ½ cup *each* whipping cream and chopped parsley
- ½ cup dry white wine or dry sherry
- ⅛ teaspoon ground nutmeg
  Salt and pepper
  About ½ cup grated Parmesan cheese

Heat oil in a wide frying pan over medium-high heat. Add onion and cook, stirring often, until lightly browned (6 to 8 minutes). Add mushrooms and continue to cook, stirring, until lightly browned. Add garlic, butter, ham, tomato, and basil; bring to a gentle boil, then reduce heat and boil gently, uncovered, for 5 minutes.

In a 5- to 6-quart pan, cook fettuccine in 3 quarts boiling water just until tender to bite (3 to 4 minutes for fresh pasta, 8 to 10 minutes for dry); or cook according to package directions. Drain well.

While fettuccine is cooking, add chicken, cream, parsley, wine, and nutmeg to mushroom-ham mixture. Mix gently until hot, then add fettuccine and mix lightly, using 2 forks. Season to taste with salt and pepper. Serve with cheese to add to taste. Makes 4 servings.

Per serving: 721 calories, 41 g protein, 42 g carbohydrates, 44 g total fat, 219 mg cholesterol, 755 mg sodium

Mexican Chicken Lasagne

Preparation time: About 30 minutes

Cooking time: About 20 minutes

Baking time: 45 to 50 minutes; 55 minutes if refrigerated

This dish certainly *looks* Italian—but when you cut into its bubbling depths, the spicy aroma lets everyone know that the flavor is Mexican.

      Chile-Cheese Filling (recipe follows)
  2   tablespoons salad oil
  1   medium-size onion, chopped
  2   cloves garlic, minced or pressed
  1   medium-size red bell pepper (about 5 oz.), seeded and chopped
  2   jars (1 lb. *each*) mild chile salsa
  ½   teaspoon pepper
  2   tablespoons chili powder
  1   teaspoon ground cumin
 10   ounces dry lasagne
  4   cups bite-size pieces cooked chicken
  1   cup (4 oz.) shredded sharp Cheddar cheese
  1   cup (4 oz.) shredded jack cheese

Prepare Chile-Cheese Filling and set aside.

Heat oil in a 4- to 5-quart pan over medium heat; add onion, garlic, and bell pepper. Cook, stirring often, until onion is soft but not brown (8 to 10 minutes). Add salsa, pepper, chili powder, and cumin; bring to a boil. Reduce heat and boil gently, uncovered, stirring often, until mixture is reduced to 1 quart (about 10 minutes).

Meanwhile, in a 5- to 6-quart pan, cook lasagne in 3 quarts boiling water just until tender to bite (about 10 minutes); or cook according to package directions. Drain, rinse with cold water, and drain well again.

Arrange half the lasagne over bottom of a 9- by 13-inch baking dish; spread with half the Chile-Cheese Filling, then cover with half the chicken. Spoon half the sauce over chicken; sprinkle with ½ cup each of the Cheddar and jack cheeses. Repeat layers, using remaining lasagne, filling, chicken, sauce, and shredded cheeses. (At this point, you may cover and refrigerate for up to 1 day.)

Bake, covered, in a 375° oven until lasagne is bubbly and hot in center (45 to 50 minutes; 55 minutes if refrigerated). Uncover and let stand for 5 minutes; cut into squares to serve. Makes 9 servings.

Chile-Cheese Filling. Combine 2 cups **small-curd cottage cheese,** 2 **eggs,** ⅓ cup chopped **parsley,** and 1 can (4 oz.) **diced green chiles.** Mix well.

Per serving: 469 calories, 36 g protein, 36 g carbohydrates, 20 g total fat, 134 mg cholesterol, 1,138 mg sodium

Chicken Carbonara

Preparation time: About 15 minutes

Cooking time: About 20 minutes

Beaten eggs, cream, and Parmesan cheese make the golden sauce that brings this creamy pasta and chicken dish together.

  ½   cup pine nuts
  4   slices bacon (about 3 oz. *total*), chopped
  8   ounces dry linguine or 1 package (9 oz.) fresh linguine
  4   eggs (room temperature)
  ½   cup grated Parmesan cheese
  ⅓   cup whipping cream
  ¼   cup chopped parsley
  ¼   cup chopped fresh basil leaves or 2 tablespoons dry basil
  3   cloves garlic, minced or pressed
 1½   cups diced cooked chicken
  1   to 2 tablespoons butter or margarine

Stir pine nuts in a wide frying pan over medium-low heat until lightly browned (about 3 minutes). Remove from pan and set aside in a large bowl. Increase heat to medium; add bacon to pan and cook until brown (about 7 minutes). Lift out bacon; place in bowl with nuts. Reserve drippings in pan.

In a 5- to 6-quart pan, cook linguine in 3 quarts boiling water just until tender to bite (8 to 10 minutes for dry pasta, 1 to 2 minutes for fresh); or cook according to package directions. Drain well.

While pasta is cooking, add eggs, cheese, cream, parsley, basil, garlic, and chicken to bacon and pine nuts. Beat until well mixed.

To reserved bacon drippings in frying pan, add enough butter to make ¼ cup; melt butter in drippings over medium heat. Add linguine, then egg mixture. Mix lightly, using 2 forks, just until linguine is well coated and heated through. Makes 4 servings.

Per serving: 662 calories, 40 g protein, 49 g carbohydrates, 35 g total fat, 306 mg cholesterol, 444 mg sodium

*Brighten the family dinner table with Spaghetti
with Turkey Parmesan (recipe on facing page): juicy, herb-
seasoned turkey patties, topped with two cheeses and
served with a simple tomato sauce and plenty of
hot pasta. Emerald-green steamed broccoli
is good alongside.*

Chicken Livers with Garlic Pasta

Preparation time: About 10 minutes

Cooking time: About 10 minutes

When time is short, try this robust dish. Hot linguine, pungent with garlic, makes a bold partner for buttery-rich sautéed chicken livers.

  6 **tablespoons butter or margarine**
  1 **pound chicken livers, drained, cut into halves**
  8 **ounces dry linguine or 1 package (9 oz.) fresh linguine**
  3 **large cloves garlic, minced or pressed**
  ½ **cup finely chopped parsley**
  ½ **teaspoon dry oregano leaves**
  ½ **cup grated Parmesan cheese (optional)**

Melt 2 tablespoons of the butter in a wide frying pan over medium-high heat. Add livers and cook, turning once, until firm and browned on outside but still pink in center; cut to test (5 to 7 minutes *total*). Keep warm.

While livers are cooking, in a 5- to 6-quart pan, cook linguine in 3 quarts boiling water just until tender to bite (8 to 10 minutes for dry pasta, 1 to 2 minutes for fresh); or cook according to package directions. Drain well.

While linguine is cooking, melt remaining ¼ cup butter in a medium-size frying pan over medium heat. Add garlic and stir until it turns opaque (1 to 2 minutes); mix in parsley and oregano.

Divide pasta among 4 warm dinner plates; drizzle with butter mixture. Arrange livers alongside. Serve with cheese, if desired. Makes 4 servings.

Per serving: 511 calories, 28 g protein, 48 g carbohydrates, 22 g total fat, 545 mg cholesterol, 270 mg sodium

Pictured on facing page

Spaghetti with Turkey Parmesan

Preparation time: About 15 minutes

Cooking time: About 50 minutes

Made with ground turkey, this colorful dish is delicious, easy to make, and certain to please the whole family.

    Tomato-Onion Sauce (recipe follows)
  1 **egg**
  ½ **cup soft bread crumbs**
 1⅓ **cups (about 7 ozs.) grated Parmesan cheese**
  ½ **teaspoon poultry seasoning**
  1 **pound ground turkey**
  1 **tablespoon butter or margarine**
  1 **tablespoon olive oil**
  4 **slices mozzarella cheese (3 oz. *total*)**
  8 **ounces dry spaghetti**
    Italian (flat-leaf) parsley sprigs (optional)

Prepare Tomato-Onion Sauce; keep warm over lowest heat.

In a medium-size bowl, beat egg until blended. Add bread crumbs, ⅓ cup of the Parmesan cheese, and poultry seasoning; stir until blended. Add turkey; mix lightly until well combined. Shape turkey mixture into 4 patties, each about 4 inches in diameter.

Melt butter in oil in a wide frying pan over medium-high heat. Add turkey patties and cook, turning once, until browned on both sides (about 8 minutes *total*). Transfer patties to a shallow rimmed baking pan or broiler pan. Spread each patty with 2 tablespoons of the Tomato-Onion Sauce; then top each with 1 slice of the mozzarella cheese and 1 tablespoon of the remaining Parmesan cheese.

Just before broiling patties, in a 5- to 6-quart pan, cook spaghetti in 3 quarts boiling water just until tender to bite (10 to 12 minutes); or cook according to package directions. Meanwhile, broil turkey patties about 4 inches below heat until cheese is melted and lightly browned (3 to 4 minutes).

Drain spaghetti well and transfer to a warm deep platter; spoon remaining Tomato-Onion Sauce over spaghetti, then top with turkey patties. Garnish with parsley sprigs, if desired. Serve with remaining ¾ cup Parmesan cheese to add to taste. Makes 4 servings.

Tomato-Onion Sauce. Heat 2 tablespoons **olive oil** or salad oil in a 2-quart pan over medium heat. Add 1 medium-size **onion,** finely chopped, 2 teaspoons **dry oregano leaves,** 1 **dry bay leaf,** and 1 large clove **garlic,** minced or pressed. Cook, stirring often, until onion is soft but not browned (about 5 minutes). Stir in 1 large can (15 oz.) **tomato sauce.** Cover, reduce heat, and simmer for 20 minutes, stirring occasionally.

Per serving: 759 calories, 47 g protein, 57 g carbohydrates, 38 g total fat, 171 mg cholesterol, 1,383 mg sodium

Polenta, Plain & Fancy

It isn't pasta, but the coarsely ground cornmeal called *polenta* is nonetheless comparable to the macaroni family in many respects. Like pasta, cooked polenta is a perfect mild-tasting foil for all kinds of flavorful sauces; next time you're hungry for simple Italian food, try topping hot polenta with Garlic Veal Stew (page 80) or the Turkey Marinara sauce on page 70.

Polenta is a staple in certain areas of northern Italy, particularly around Venice and in the regions of Piedmont and Lombardy. In rural markets, you may see flaring, bell-shaped copper or brass pots specifically designed for cooking polenta. Old-time cooks stirred the slowly bubbling mush with a wooden spoon or stick until it was thick enough to pull from the sides of the pan—and to hold the spoon firmly upright!

Today, though, there's more than one way to cook traditional-tasting polenta. You can still use the old-fashioned method, of course—but if you'd rather not stand over the polenta, stirring it constantly, try our microwaved or baked versions of the standard recipe. We also offer some fresh new ways to present polenta—in rich, cheese-dappled cakes to accompany grilled sausages or chops, for example, or as the crust of a savory cheese tart to serve with a crisp green salad.

Stove-top Polenta

3½ cups regular-strength chicken broth or water
1 cup polenta (Italian-style cornmeal) or yellow cornmeal
Salt and pepper

In a deep 4- to 5-quart pan, bring 2 cups of the broth to a boil over high heat. Meanwhile, mix polenta with remaining 1½ cups broth. Stir polenta mixture into boiling broth. Return mixture to a boil, stirring often. When spatters of polenta cannot be stirred down, reduce heat so mixture boils very slowly. Cook until reduced to about 3 cups, stirring constantly to prevent scorching as polenta thickens. Total cooking time is 15 to 20 minutes, starting from the time polenta first boils. Season to taste with salt and pepper.

To serve as is, spoon into a mound on a board or platter; let stand for 5 to 10 minutes to firm up slightly, then cut or slice to serve. Or use in the following recipes. Makes 4 to 6 servings.

Per serving: 103 calories, 3 g protein, 19 g carbohydrates, 2 g total fat, 0 mg cholesterol, 586 mg sodium

Gorgonzola Polenta Cakes

3 tablespoons olive oil
1 small onion, finely chopped
1 clove garlic, minced or pressed
2 tablespoons finely chopped parsley
  Stove-top Polenta (at left)
¼ cup grated Parmesan cheese
⅓ cup crumbled Gorgonzola or other blue-veined cheese
1 egg, beaten just to blend

Heat 1 tablespoon of the oil in a wide frying pan over medium heat. Add onion and cook, stirring often, until soft but not brown (about 5 minutes). Add garlic and stir until opaque. Remove pan from heat and stir in parsley; set aside.

Prepare Stove-top Polenta, but omit salt. Into warm polenta, stir onion mixture, Parmesan cheese, and Gorgonzola cheese. Let stand for at least 5 minutes to firm up slightly. Blend in egg.

Heat remaining 2 tablespoons oil in a wide nonstick frying pan over medium heat. Scoop out polenta, using a scant ½ cup for each portion, and slide into oil; flatten slightly to make round patties. Don't crowd pan (you can cook about 4 patties at a time). Cook patties, turning carefully once, until browned on both sides (10 to 12 minutes total). Makes 8 patties (4 to 8 servings).

Per patty: 165 calories, 5 g protein, 15 g carbohydrates, 9 g total fat, 33 mg cholesterol, 572 mg sodium

Polenta Cheese Tart

½ recipe Stove-top Polenta (at left)
1¼ cups (about 6 oz.) crumbled goat cheese, such as Bûcheron or Montrachet, or 1 cup (about 4 oz.) ½-inch cubes cream cheese
1 cup (about 4 oz.) crumbled blue-veined cheese or shredded provolone cheese
1 cup (4 oz.) shredded mozzarella cheese
⅓ cup thinly sliced green onions (including tops)

Prepare Stove-top Polenta, using 1¾ cups broth or water and ½ cup polenta (start with 1 cup of the broth in a 2- to 3-quart pan; mix polenta with remaining ¾ cup broth). Cook until reduced to 1 to 1½ cups (7 to 10 minutes). Omit salt.

Pour polenta into a greased 7½- to 8-inch tart pan with a removable bottom. Let stand until just cool enough to touch; with fingers, press polenta evenly over bottom and up pan sides. Mix goat, blue, and mozzarella cheeses (or cream, provolone, and mozzarella cheeses) with onions; spoon into polenta shell. Bake, uncovered, in a 350° oven until mozzarella cheese is melted (about 30 minutes). Carefully remove pan sides and cut tart into wedges. Makes 6 servings.

Per serving: 276 calories, 15 g protein, 13 g carbohydrates, 18 g total fat, 55·mg cholesterol, 802 mg sodium

Microwave Polenta

2 cups regular-strength chicken broth or water
½ cup polenta (Italian-style cornmeal) or yellow cornmeal
1 tablespoon butter or margarine
Salt (optional)
¼ to ⅓ cup grated Parmesan cheese

In a 2-quart microwave-safe measuring cup or bowl, stir together broth, polenta, and butter. Microwave, uncovered, on **HIGH (100%)** for 12 to 15 minutes or until polenta is tender and liquid has been absorbed, stirring at 5-minute intervals. Spoon polènta into a serving dish; season to taste with salt, if desired. Serve with cheese to add to taste. Makes about 3 servings.

Per serving: 175 calories, 7 g protein, 20 g carbohydrates, 8 g total fat, 16 mg cholesterol, 853 mg sodium

Baked Polenta

5 cups regular-strength chicken broth
1½ cups polenta (Italian-style cornmeal) or yellow cornmeal
1 small onion, finely chopped
¼ cup butter or margarine, diced
½ to ¾ cup grated Parmesan cheese

In a greased 9- by 13-inch baking dish (rectangular or oval), stir together

broth, polenta, onion, and butter. Bake, uncovered, in a 350° oven until liquid has been absorbed (45 to 50 minutes). Serve with cheese to add to taste. Makes 6 servings.

Per serving: 261 calories, 8 g protein, 30 g carbohydrates, 12 g total fat, 27 mg cholesterol, 1,072 mg sodium

Baked Polenta & Sausages

5 medium-size red bell peppers (about 1¾ lbs. *total*), seeded and cut into large slices
12 ounces mushrooms, sliced about ¼ inch thick
1½ pounds mild or hot Italian sausages
Baked Polenta (at left)
2 cups (8 oz.) shredded jack cheese

Spread bell peppers and mushrooms in a shallow 9- by 13-inch baking dish (rectangular or oval). Pierce each sausage in several places with a fork; lay sausages atop vegetables. Bake, uncovered, in a 350° oven for 10 to 15 minutes.

Meanwhile, stir together Baked Polenta mixture in its own greased baking dish.

When sausage mixture has baked for 10 to 15 minutes, stir vegetables to moisten with pan drippings and add polenta to oven. Bake until sausages are lightly browned and no longer pink in center (cut to test) and polenta has absorbed liquid (45 to 50 more minutes). Sprinkle polenta with jack cheese (omit Parmesan cheese called for in Baked Polenta recipe).

Serve polenta and sausage mixture from baking dishes; or spoon polenta into center of a warm deep platter and surround with sausage mixture. Makes 6 servings.

Per serving: 837 calories, 36 g protein, 39 g carbohydrates, 60 g total fat, 147 mg cholesterol, 2,109 mg sodium

Saucy Chicken & Baked Polenta

8 chicken thighs (2 to 2½ lbs. *total*)
1 small onion, finely chopped
1 small green bell pepper (about 4 oz.), seeded and chopped
1 can (14½ oz. to 1 lb.) stewed tomatoes
1 can (8 oz.) tomato sauce
½ cup dry red wine
2 teaspoons dry oregano leaves
1 teaspoon dry basil
Baked Polenta (at left)
¼ to ⅓ cup grated Parmesan cheese

Rinse chicken pieces, pat dry, and arrange slightly apart in a 9- by 13-inch baking pan. Broil about 4 inches below heat, turning once, until browned on both sides (12 to 14 minutes *total*). Lift chicken from pan and set aside. To pan, add onion, bell pepper, tomatoes, tomato sauce, wine, oregano, and basil; mix well.

Stir together Baked Polenta mixture in a greased 9-inch square baking pan or baking dish, using 3½ cups broth and 1 cup polenta; omit onion and butter.

Place baking pans with vegetable mixture and polenta in a 450° oven. Bake, uncovered, stirring both mixtures once or twice, until vegetables are very soft and have formed a thick sauce and polenta liquid is almost absorbed (35 to 40 minutes).

Place chicken pieces in vegetable sauce. Sprinkle cheese over polenta. Continue to bake both mixtures, uncovered, until chicken is no longer pink near bone; cut to test (about 10 more minutes). Serve chicken and sauce over portions of polenta. Makes 4 to 8 servings.

Per serving: 552 calories, 30 g protein, 39 g carbohydrates, 31 g total fat, 128 mg cholesterol, 1,561 mg sodium

Turkey Marinara with Perciatelli

Preparation time: About 20 minutes

Cooking time: About 1¾ hours

The flavor of this thick, chunky tomato sauce will satisfy any traditionalist, but it's made with browned ground turkey (not beef) and a host of fresh vegetables. Serve it over *perciatelli*—long, thin pasta tubes.

>   2 tablespoons olive oil
>   1 medium-size onion, finely chopped
>   1 medium-size green bell pepper (about 5 oz.), seeded and finely chopped
>   2 medium-size carrots (about 4 oz. *total*), finely shredded
>   4 ounces mushrooms, thinly sliced
>   2 tablespoons chopped parsley
>   1 clove garlic, minced or pressed
>   2 teaspoons dry basil leaves
>   1 teaspoon *each* dry rosemary and dry oregano leaves
>   1 pound ground turkey
>   2 large cans (28 oz. *each*) pear-shaped tomatoes
>   1 large can (12 oz.) tomato paste
>   ¼ cup dry red wine
>   1 dry bay leaf
>   Salt and pepper
>   1 pound dry perciatelli or spaghetti
>   About 1 cup (about 5 oz.) grated Parmesan cheese

Heat oil in a 4- to 5-quart pan over medium-high heat. Add onion, bell pepper, carrots, mushrooms, parsley, garlic, basil, rosemary, and oregano. Cook, stirring often, until vegetables are tender to bite (about 15 minutes). Lift vegetables from pan, transfer to a bowl, and set aside.

Crumble turkey into pan; cook over medium-high heat, stirring constantly, until juices have evaporated. Return vegetables to pan and continue to cook, stirring, until turkey is lightly browned. Add tomatoes (break up with a spoon) and their liquid, tomato paste, wine, and bay leaf, stirring to scrape up browned bits from bottom of pan.

Increase heat to high and bring mixture to a boil; reduce heat to medium-low, cover, and boil gently, stirring often, for 30 minutes. Then uncover and continue to cook, stirring occasionally, until sauce is reduced to 8 to 10 cups (40 to 50 more minutes). Season to taste with salt and pepper.

Shortly before sauce is done, in a 6- to 8-quart pan, cook perciatelli in 4 quarts boiling water just until tender to bite (12 to 15 minutes); or cook according to package directions. Drain well and transfer to a warm large serving bowl. Top with sauce and mix lightly, using 2 spoons. Serve with cheese to add to taste. Makes 8 to 10 servings.

Per serving: 419 calories, 23 g protein, 57 g carbohydrates, 12 g total fat, 41 mg cholesterol, 805 mg sodium

Pictured on facing page

Turkey with Tortellini & Oranges

Preparation time: About 25 minutes

Cooking time: About 20 minutes

When you're lucky enough to have plenty of cold roast turkey, dice or shred some of it to use in this elegant pasta dish. Turkey and tortellini are bathed in a sour cream sauce and garnished with gleaming orange slices.

>   3 large oranges (about 1½ lbs. *total*)
>   7 cups regular-strength chicken broth
>   1½ pounds fresh cheese- or meat-filled plain or spinach tortellini
>   3 cups diced or shredded cooked turkey
>   2 teaspoons celery seeds
>   2 cups sour cream
>   ¼ cup chopped chives

Using a vegetable peeler, cut a strip of peel (colored part only) 6 inches long and about 1 inch wide from one of the oranges. Cut strip into long, thin shreds and set aside. Then completely peel all 3 oranges, discarding peel and all white membrane. Cut each orange crosswise into 6 slices; set slices aside.

In a 5- to 6-quart pan, bring broth to a boil. Add tortellini and cook just until tender to bite (4 to 6 minutes; or cook according to package directions). With a slotted spoon, lift out tortellini and transfer to a warm platter; keep warm.

To broth in pan, add turkey, celery seeds, and orange peel shreds; cook just until turkey is heated through. Lift out turkey and spoon over tortellini. Place sour cream in a small pan, then stir in 3 tablespoons of the chives and ½ cup of the hot broth (reserve remaining broth for other uses). Stir broth–sour cream mixture over low heat just until hot, then spoon over turkey. Sprinkle with remaining 1 tablespoon chives; arrange orange slices around turkey and pasta. Makes 6 servings.

Per serving: 706 calories, 45 g protein, 71 g carbohydrates, 28 g total fat, 150 mg cholesterol, 1,772 mg sodium

*Plump little cheese-filled pasta rings and fresh
orange slices give leftover poultry a sophisticated new
look. When you make Turkey with Tortellini & Oranges
(recipe on facing page), take your choice of green
or golden pasta.*

Cavatappi

Pea Pod & Turkey Pasta

Preparation time: About 10 minutes

Cooking time: About 10 minutes

Here's a quick pasta combination that can be made on the range or in the microwave with equally delicious results.

- 1 package (9 oz.) fresh fettuccine
- 1 can (14½ oz.) regular-strength chicken broth
- 1 cup whipping cream
- ⅛ teaspoon ground nutmeg
- 2 cups diced cooked turkey
- 1 package (6 oz.) frozen Chinese pea pods, thawed and drained
- 2 cups (8 oz.) shredded Swiss cheese
  Salt and pepper

In a 5- to 6-quart pan, cook fettuccine in 3 quarts boiling water until not quite tender to bite (about 3 minutes); or cook for about 1 minute less than time specified in package directions. Drain well.

While pasta is cooking, combine broth, cream, and nutmeg in a wide frying pan. Bring to a full boil over high heat. Boil, stirring often, until mixture is reduced to 1½ cups (6 to 8 minutes). Reduce heat to medium and add turkey, pea pods, and pasta; mix lightly, using 2 forks. Sprinkle evenly with cheese. Heat without stirring just until cheese is melted (2 to 3 minutes). Season to taste with salt and pepper. Makes 4 to 6 servings.

Per serving: 580 calories, 39 g protein, 34 g carbohydrates, 32 g total fat, 198 mg cholesterol, 555 mg sodium

■ *To Microwave:* Spread fettuccine in a shallow 2- to 2½-quart microwave-safe casserole. Pour broth and cream over fettuccine; sprinkle with nutmeg. Microwave, covered, on **HIGH (100%)** for about 9 minutes or until pasta is tender to bite, stirring every 3 minutes. Mix in turkey and microwave, uncovered, on **HIGH (100%)** for 2 minutes. Add pea pods and cheese; mix lightly, using 2 forks, until blended. Microwave, covered, on **HIGH (100%)** for 1 to 2 minutes or just until cheese is melted. Season to taste with salt and pepper.

Turkey alla Cacciatora

Preparation time: About 30 minutes

Cooking time: 1¾ to 2¼ hours

In Italian cooking, the word *cacciatora* refers to poultry or meat cooked "hunter's style"—with the bold flavors preferred for preparing game. To make our sturdy dish, however, you need only hunt down a few pounds of dark meat turkey parts, such as thighs, drumsticks, or hindquarters.

- 4 pounds turkey thighs, drumsticks, or hindquarters
- 2 tablespoons olive oil
- 3 large onions, chopped
- 4 cloves garlic, minced or pressed
- 2 medium-size green bell peppers (10 to 12 oz. *total*), seeded and chopped
- 8 ounces mushrooms, sliced
- 2 tablespoons all-purpose flour
- 1 can (8 oz.) tomato sauce
- 1 can (14½ oz. to 1 lb.) tomatoes
- ½ cup *each* dry red wine and regular-strength chicken broth
- ½ teaspoon salt
- 1 teaspoon *each* dry basil, dry thyme leaves, and dry oregano leaves
- 1 tablespoon sugar
- ⅛ teaspoon ground allspice
- 2 dry bay leaves
- 1 pound dry spaghetti or vermicelli (not coil vermicelli)
- 2 tablespoons butter or margarine, melted
- 2 tablespoons finely chopped parsley
  About 1 cup (about 5 oz.) grated Parmesan cheese

Rinse turkey pieces and pat dry. Heat oil in a wide, heavy 6- to 8-quart pan over medium-high heat. Add turkey; cook, turning as needed, until browned on all sides. Lift out and set aside.

Add onions to pan and cook, stirring often, until soft but not brown (8 to 10 minutes). Stir in garlic, bell peppers, and mushrooms; continue to cook, stirring, until almost all liquid has evaporated. Sprinkle flour over vegetable mixture, then stir in well. Add tomato sauce, tomatoes (break up with a spoon) and their liquid, wine, broth, salt, basil, thyme, oregano, sugar, allspice, and bay leaves. Bring to a boil, stirring often.

Return turkey to pan, pushing pieces down into sauce. Reduce heat, cover, and simmer for 30 minutes. Then uncover and continue to cook, stirring occasionally and adjusting heat so mixture barely bubbles, until turkey is very tender when pierced (1 to 1½ more hours).

About 15 minutes before turkey is done, in a 6- to 8-quart pan, cook spaghetti in 4 quarts boiling water just until tender to bite (10 to 12 minutes); or cook according to package directions. Drain well, then transfer to a warm large serving bowl; mix lightly with butter and parsley.

Spoon turkey and sauce over spaghetti. Sprinkle with ⅓ cup of the cheese. Serve with remaining cheese to add to taste. Makes 8 servings.

Per serving: 654 calories, 46 g protein, 59 g carbohydrates, 25 g total fat, 137 mg cholesterol, 795 mg sodium

Pictured on page 2

Barbecued Quail with Pappardelle in Mushroom Sauce

Preparation time: About 20 minutes

Cooking time: About 30 minutes

Grilling time: 8 to 10 minutes

Look for fresh or frozen quail in the poultry section of your supermarket. The little all-dark-meat birds grill to sizzling perfection in about 10 minutes; while they cook, you boil the ribbonlike pasta to serve with fresh tomato-mushroom sauce.

If you prefer, you can use Rock Cornish game hens in place of quail, allowing one or two halves for each serving (see *Note* below).

      2 ounces sliced pancetta or bacon, diced
      6 tablespoons olive oil
      1 medium-size onion, thinly sliced
      8 ounces mushrooms, quartered
      2 cloves garlic, minced or pressed
      6 medium-size pear-shaped (Roma-type) tomatoes (about 12 oz. *total*), chopped
      ¼ cup slivered fresh sage leaves or 2 teaspoons dry sage
      1 cup dry white wine
      8 quail (3 to 4 oz. *each*), thawed if frozen
         Coarsely ground pepper
      1 package (8½ oz.) dry pappardelle (wide fettuccine), 10 to 12 ounces fresh pappardelle, or 8 ounces dry extra-wide egg noodles
         Salt
         Fresh sage sprigs
         Lemon wedges (optional)

In a wide frying pan, cook pancetta over medium heat until crisp. Lift out, drain, and set aside. To pan drippings, add ¼ cup of the oil, then onion and

mushrooms. Increase heat to medium-high and cook, stirring often, until mushrooms are lightly browned (about 5 minutes). Stir in garlic, tomatoes, slivered sage, and wine. Adjust heat so mixture boils gently. Cook, uncovered, stirring occasionally, until tomatoes are soft and sauce is slightly thickened (10 to 15 minutes).

Meanwhile, cut through backbone of each quail with poultry shears or a knife. Place quail, skin side up, on a flat surface; press down firmly, cracking bones slightly, until birds lie flat. Rinse quail, pat dry, and brush well on all sides with remaining 2 tablespoons oil; sprinkle with pepper.

Place birds, skin side up, on a lightly greased grill 4 to 6 inches above a solid bed of hot coals. Cook, turning occasionally, until skin is browned and breast meat is still pink at bone; cut to test (8 to 10 minutes *total*). Remove from grill and keep warm.

In a 5- to 6-quart pan, cook pasta in 3 quarts boiling water just until barely tender to bite (3 to 4 minutes for dry pappardelle, about 2 minutes for fresh pappardelle, 4 to 6 minutes for noodles); or cook according to package directions. Drain well.

Add pancetta to tomato sauce; season to taste with salt. Add pasta and mix lightly, using 2 spoons. Transfer to a warm large platter. Surround pasta with grilled quail. Garnish with sage sprigs and lemon wedges, if desired. Makes 4 servings.

Per serving: 874 calories, 46 g protein, 52 g carbohydrates, 53 g total fat, 66 mg cholesterol, 207 mg sodium

Note: To prepare with Rock Cornish game hens, use 2 or 4 hens (1¼ to 1½ lbs. *each*). Remove necks and giblets; reserve for other uses, if desired. Rinse hens and pat dry. Cut each hen in half, cutting through backbone and breastbone. Brush with olive oil and season with pepper as directed for quail. Grill over medium (not hot) coals. Cook, turning several times, until meat near thighbone is no longer pink; cut to test (30 to 40 minutes). Surround pasta mixture with grilled game hen halves.

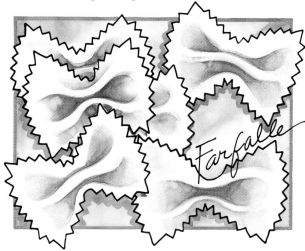

Tender round steak swirled around a filling of raisins,
parsley, garlic, and cheese makes the savory centerpiece
for hearty Braciola & Meatballs with Fusilli
(recipe on facing page).

Meats

By some quirk of cultural migration, pasta reached the New World from Italy in the form of spaghetti and meatballs—a match-up far less common on its supposed home ground than its popularity here would suggest. But as anyone who first discovered spaghetti in that guise will attest, it's an inspired combination. Equally captivating, though, are many other pairings of meat and pasta. Serve jaunty bow-shaped noodles with a braised pot roast of beef as a change from the usual potatoes; accompany a vibrant veal stew with plump agnolotti or ravioli. Stir up a speedy sausage sauce to spoon over thin strands of vermicelli. Or bake a casserole of tender pork chops layered with a dressing of tiny pasta stars and colorful vegetables.

Pictured on facing page

Braciola & Meatballs with Fusilli

Preparation time: About 30 minutes

Cooking time: About 2 hours and 20 minutes

Three kinds of meat—sausages, raisin-studded meatballs, and a savory rolled steak—are simmered in a rich red sauce, then served over hot fusilli or spaghetti in this pasta extravaganza. The recipe serves 8 to 12 people generously.

> **Braciola (page 76)**
> **Raisin Meatballs (page 76)**
> 1 **pound mild Italian sausages (optional)**
> **About ¼ cup salad oil**
> 1 **small onion, finely chopped**
> 2 **cloves garlic, minced or pressed**
> 1 **large can (15 oz.) tomato sauce**
> 3 **cups water**
> 1 **large can (12 oz.) tomato paste**
> 3 **dry bay leaves**
> ¼ **teaspoon crushed dried hot red chiles**
> 2 **tablespoons coarsely chopped fresh basil or 1 tablespoon dry basil**
> **Salt**
> 1½ **pounds long fusilli or spaghetti**
> **Fresh herb sprigs, such as parsley, thyme, and oregano (optional)**

Prepare Braciola and Raisin Meatballs; set aside.

If using Italian sausages, prick each several times with a fork; then cut each in half (or into 3-inch lengths). Then place in a 6-quart or larger pan over medium heat; brown on all sides and remove from pan. Add 1 to 2 tablespoons of the oil, if needed; then add Braciola and brown well on all sides. Remove from pan. Then brown meatballs, about half at a time, adding more oil as needed; remove meatballs from pan as they are browned.

Add onion and garlic to pan; cook, stirring often, until soft. Stir in tomato sauce, 3 cups water, tomato paste, bay leaves, and chiles. Return Braciola to pan. Reduce heat, cover, and simmer for 1 hour. Then add meatballs, sausages, and basil; continue to simmer, covered, until Braciola is tender when pierced (about 1 more hour). Season sauce to taste with salt.

When meat is almost tender, in an 8- to 10-quart pan, cook fusilli in 5 quarts boiling water just until tender to bite (12 to 15 minutes); or cook according to package directions. Drain well.

Lift meats from sauce. Remove cord from Braciola and cut meat crosswise into thick slices. Arrange slices in center of a warm large, deep platter. Surround with fusilli. Arrange sausages and meatballs over fusilli. Pour about a fourth of the sauce over meats and fusilli. Garnish with a bouquet of herb sprigs, if desired. Serve remaining sauce to add to taste. Makes 8 to 12 servings.

Braciola. Remove and discard fat and bone from 1 **round steak** (about 1½ lbs.). Using the flat side of a mallet, pound meat between 2 pieces of plastic wrap until flattened to about ½ inch thick. Spread with 1 tablespoon **butter** or margarine (at room temperature). Sprinkle with ½ cup chopped **parsley,** 2 tablespoons grated **Parmesan cheese,** 2 cloves **garlic** (minced or pressed), **pepper** to taste, and ½ cup **raisins.** Starting with a short edge, roll meat up jelly roll style. Tie with cord at about 1½-inch intervals.

Raisin Meatballs. In a medium-size bowl, beat 1 **egg.** Add 1 pound **lean ground beef,** 1 small **onion** (finely chopped), ½ cup chopped **parsley,** 2 cloves **garlic** (minced or pressed), and ½ cup **raisins.** Mix lightly, then shape into 1½-inch balls.

Per serving: 607 calories, 32 g protein, 74 g carbohydrates, 21 g total fat, 89 mg cholesterol, 629 mg sodium

Wine-braised Chuck Roast with Bow Ties

Preparation time: About 15 minutes

Baking time: 2½ to 3 hours

Cooking time: About 20 minutes

A boneless beef roast bakes to moist tenderness in a spicy tomato sauce that's also delicious with the accompanying pasta. Sprinkle fresh mint over all just before serving.

- 2 **tablespoons olive oil or salad oil**
- 1 **large onion, finely chopped**
- 4 **cloves garlic, slivered**
- 1 **cup** *each* **dry red wine and water**
- 1 **can (8 oz.) tomato sauce**
- 2 **tablespoons red wine vinegar**
- 1 **dry bay leaf**
- 5 **whole allspice**
- 1 **cinnamon stick (about 3 inches long)**
- 1 **teaspoon cumin seeds**
- ½ **teaspoon** *each* **salt and pepper**
- 1 **boneless beef chuck roast (3 to 3½ lbs.), trimmed of fat**
- 12 **ounces dry bow-shaped pasta**
- 2 **to 3 tablespoons chopped fresh mint leaves**

Heat oil in a wide frying pan over medium heat. Add onion and garlic; cook, stirring often, until onion is soft but not brown (6 to 8 minutes). Stir in wine, water, tomato sauce, vinegar, bay leaf, allspice, cinnamon stick, cumin seeds, salt, and pepper. Increase heat to high and bring mixture to a boil; then remove from heat.

Place roast in a 9- by 13-inch baking pan; pour sauce over it. Cover with foil and bake in a 325° oven until meat is very tender when pierced (2½ to 3 hours). Slice roast and arrange in center of a warm deep platter; keep warm. Skim and discard fat from sauce; remove and discard bay leaf and cinnamon stick. Transfer sauce to a 2- to 3-quart pan. Bring to a boil over high heat; boil, stirring often, until reduced to 2 cups (about 10 minutes).

Meanwhile, in a 6- to 8-quart pan, cook pasta in 4 quarts boiling water just until tender to bite (about 10 minutes); or cook according to package directions. Drain well and spoon around meat; pour sauce over pasta and meat, then sprinkle mint over all. Makes 6 to 8 servings.

Per serving: 539 calories, 40 g protein, 41 g carbohydrates, 23 g total fat, 158 mg cholesterol, 491 mg sodium

Lasagne with Spinach

Preparation time: About 15 minutes

Cooking time: About 15 minutes

Baking time: About 1 hour and 10 minutes

This hearty entrée can be put together especially quickly, since the pasta cooks as the lasagne bakes—there's no need to boil it before you assemble the casserole.

- 8 ounces lean ground beef
- 3 cans (15 oz. *each*) marinara sauce
- ½ cup *each* water and dry red wine
- ¼ teaspoon *each* dry basil and dry oregano leaves
- 1 package (10 oz.) frozen chopped spinach, thawed
- 8 ounces ricotta cheese
- ¾ cup grated Parmesan cheese
- 2 eggs
- ⅛ teaspoon ground nutmeg
  Salt and pepper
- 8 ounces dry lasagne
- 12 ounces mozzarella cheese, sliced

Crumble beef into a wide frying pan over medium heat; cook, stirring, until browned (5 to 8 minutes). Spoon off and discard excess fat. Stir in marinara sauce, water, wine, basil, and oregano. Bring to a boil; boil gently, uncovered, stirring often, for 5 minutes. Set aside.

Squeeze as much liquid as possible from spinach. In a food processor or blender, combine spinach, ricotta cheese, ½ cup of the Parmesan cheese, eggs, and nutmeg; whirl until well combined. Season to taste with salt and pepper.

To assemble casserole, rinse dry lasagne well. Then spoon about a fifth of the meat sauce into a 9- by 13-inch baking dish. Cover with a third of the lasagne. Add another fifth of the meat sauce, half the remaining lasagne, and another fifth of the meat sauce. Cover with half of the mozzarella slices; spread with spinach mixture and top with remaining mozzarella slices. Add half the remaining sauce, remaining lasagne, and remaining sauce.

Cover and bake in a 375° oven for 1 hour. Uncover, sprinkle with remaining ¼ cup Parmesan cheese, and continue to bake, uncovered, until lasagne is tender when pierced (about 10 more minutes). Let stand for several minutes before cutting. Makes 8 servings.

Per serving: 491 calories, 28 g protein, 42 g carbohydrates, 25 g total fat, 118 mg cholesterol, 1,396 mg sodium

Agnolotti

Beef-Mushroom Spaghetti in Barbecue Sauce

Preparation time: About 20 minutes

Cooking time: 20 to 25 minutes

If it's too late in the year for outdoor cooking but you still have a bottle of barbecue sauce lingering in the fridge, you're in luck. You can use it to make this easy spaghetti sauce with ground beef and plenty of mushrooms.

- 1 pound lean ground beef
  Salad oil (optional)
- 12 ounces mushrooms, sliced
- 2 medium-size onions, finely chopped
- 1 medium-size green bell pepper (about 5 oz.), seeded and finely chopped
- 1 teaspoon dry oregano leaves
- 8 ounces dry spaghetti
- 1¼ cups prepared tomato-based barbecue sauce
  Chopped parsley

Crumble beef into a wide 3- to 4-quart pan over medium heat; cook, stirring, until browned (10 to 15 minutes). Add up to 2 tablespoons oil, if necessary; or spoon off and discard all but 2 tablespoons of the fat. Add mushrooms, onions, bell pepper, and oregano; cook, stirring often, until onion is soft and lightly browned (about 10 minutes).

Meanwhile, in a 5- to 6-quart pan, cook spaghetti in 3 quarts boiling water just until tender to bite (10 to 12 minutes); or cook according to package directions. Drain well.

Add spaghetti and barbecue sauce to beef mixture; mix lightly, using 2 forks, just until heated through. Sprinkle with parsley. Makes 6 servings.

Per serving: 436 calories, 20 g protein, 53 g carbohydrates, 17 g total fat, 51 mg cholesterol, 888 mg sodium

Spicy Mediterranean Meatballs

Preparation time: About 45 minutes

Cooking time: About 1 hour and 20 minutes

Fresh mint, cilantro, and a blend of sweet spices give meatballs in tomato sauce a Mediterranean character.

> Herbed Meatballs (recipe follows)
>
> 3   tablespoons salad oil
>
> 2   medium-size onions, finely chopped
>
> 3   cloves garlic, minced or pressed
>
> 1   teaspoon *each* minced fresh ginger and ground cumin
>
> 1   tablespoon paprika
>
> ¼   cup finely chopped fresh cilantro (coriander) or parsley
>
> 3   tablespoons red wine vinegar
>
> 2   large tomatoes (about 12 oz. *total*), peeled and chopped
>
> 1   can (14½ oz.) regular-strength beef broth
>
> 1   beef bouillon cube
>
> 1   can (6 oz.) tomato paste
>
> 1   pound dry spaghetti
>
> 1   cup (about 5 oz.) grated Parmesan cheese

Prepare Herbed Meatballs and set aside.

Heat oil in a wide frying pan over medium-high heat. Add onions and cook, stirring, until they begin to soften (about 5 minutes). Stir in garlic, ginger, cumin, paprika, cilantro, vinegar, tomatoes, broth, and bouillon cube. Increase heat to high and cook, stirring, until mixture comes to a boil. Add meatballs; reduce heat, cover, and simmer for 1 hour.

Lift meatballs carefully from sauce and keep warm. Add tomato paste to sauce; increase heat to high and cook, stirring often, until sauce is thickened (about 10 more minutes).

Meanwhile, in a 6- to 8-quart pan, cook spaghetti in 4 quarts boiling water just until tender to bite (10 to 12 minutes); or cook according to package directions. Drain well, transfer to a warm deep platter, and top with meatballs. Spoon sauce over spaghetti and meatballs. Serve with cheese to add to taste. Makes 8 servings.

Herbed Meatballs. Crumble 1½ pounds **lean ground beef** into a large bowl. Add ¼ cup **fine dry bread crumbs,** 3 **eggs,** and 1 large **onion,** finely chopped; mix well. Sprinkle with ¼ cup finely chopped **fresh cilantro** (coriander) or parsley, ¼ cup finely chopped **fresh mint,** 1 tablespoon

paprika, 1 teaspoon **salt,** ½ teaspoon **pepper,** and ¼ teaspoon **ground cloves;** mix lightly until thoroughly combined. Shape into 1-inch balls.

Per serving: 620 calories, 32 g protein, 56 g carbohydrates, 29 g total fat, 152 mg cholesterol, 1,026 mg sodium

Norwegian Meatballs with Gjetost Sauce

Preparation time: About 20 minutes

Baking time: About 15 minutes

Cooking time: About 10 minutes

Here's an unusual version of pasta and meatballs. The delicately flavored sauce features *gjetost*, a firm, caramel-colored Norwegian cheese with a distinctive, rather sweet flavor. Look for 8-ounce bricks of gjetost in the supermarket dairy case.

> 1   egg
>
> ¼   cup all-purpose flour
>
> 1   pound ground veal or lean ground beef (or 8 oz. of *each* meat)
>
> 1   cup regular-strength chicken broth
>
> ½   cup half-and-half or milk
>
> ¾   cup shredded gjetost cheese
>
> ½   cup sour cream
>
> 1   tablespoon chopped fresh dill or ½ teaspoon dry dill weed
>
>   Salt and ground white pepper
>
> 1   package (9 oz.) fresh linguine

In a medium-size bowl, beat egg with flour. Lightly mix in veal and ½ cup of the broth until well combined. Shape mixture into 1-inch balls; place slightly apart in a greased shallow baking pan. Bake, uncovered, in a 450° oven until well browned (about 15 minutes). Using a spatula, loosen meatballs from pan; set aside in pan and keep warm.

In a wide frying pan, combine half-and-half and remaining ½ cup broth; bring to steaming over medium heat (do not boil). Add cheese and stir until melted. Reduce heat to low and stir in sour cream and dill until smooth. Lightly mix in meatballs and any pan drippings; season to taste with salt and white pepper. Keep warm over lowest heat.

In a 5- to 6-quart pan, cook linguine in 3 quarts boiling water just until tender to bite (1 to 2 minutes); or cook according to package directions. Drain well, divide among warm dinner plates, and top with meatballs in sauce. Makes 4 servings.

Per serving: 604 calories, 37 g protein, 53 g carbohydrates, 27 g total fat, 245 mg cholesterol, 533 mg sodium

The dish may look familiar, but the flavor's far from traditional! Spicy Mediterranean Meatballs (recipe on facing page) forego the typical oregano and basil for ginger, cumin, cilantro, cloves, and plenty of fresh mint.

Green Lasagne Donatello

Preparation time: About 20 minutes

Cooking time: About 1 hour

Baking time: 50 minutes; 1 hour and 5 minutes if refrigerated

Your own homemade spinach pasta, a subtly flavored cream sauce, and a thick tomato-veal sauce add up to a delectable and unusual dish.

- 1 recipe Spinach Pasta (page 6)
- 2 tablespoons butter or margarine
- 2 tablespoons olive oil
- ½ cup *each* finely chopped onion, celery, and carrot
- 1 pound ground veal
- 1 cup dry white wine
- 1 can (14½ oz.) pear-shaped tomatoes
- 2 tablespoons tomato paste
- ½ cup whipping cream
  Cream Sauce (recipe follows)
- 1 cup (about 5 oz.) grated Parmesan cheese
- 8 ounces mozzarella cheese, thinly sliced

After rolling out Spinach Pasta, cut strips so they are about as long as a shallow 3-quart casserole or 9- by 13-inch baking dish; cover lightly and set aside.

Melt butter in oil in a wide frying pan over medium heat. Add onion, celery, and carrot; cook, stirring often, until onion is soft but not brown (about 10 minutes). Crumble in veal and continue to cook, stirring, until meat loses its pink color. Add wine; bring to a boil and cook, stirring often, until liquid has evaporated. Add tomatoes (break up with a spoon) and their liquid, tomato paste, and cream; continue to cook, uncovered, until sauce is reduced to 1 quart (about 15 minutes).

Prepare Cream Sauce and set aside.

In a 6- to 8-quart pan, cook pasta, 2 strips at a time, in 4 quarts boiling water just until tender to bite (2 to 3 minutes). As pasta is cooked, lift it from pan and transfer to a bowl of ice water to cool.

Drain pasta strips, one at a time; pat dry. Arrange a third of the strips, overlapping slightly, in casserole. Spread with a third of the Cream Sauce, then a third of the veal sauce; sprinkle with a third of the Parmesan cheese, then layer on half the mozzarella cheese. Add another layer of pasta, Cream Sauce, veal sauce, and Parmesan cheese. Then add remaining ingredients in this order: pasta, veal sauce, mozzarella cheese, Cream Sauce, and Parmesan cheese. (At this point, you may cover and refrigerate for up to 1 day.)

Bake, uncovered, in a 400° oven until lightly browned and heated through (about 50 minutes; about 1 hour and 5 minutes if refrigerated). Let stand for several minutes before cutting. Makes 10 servings.

Cream Sauce. Melt ½ cup (¼ lb.) **butter** or margarine in a 2-quart pan over medium heat. Blend in ½ cup **all-purpose flour**; stir until bubbly. Remove from heat; gradually stir in 2 cups *each* **regular-strength chicken broth** and **half-and-half**. Return to heat; cook, stirring, until sauce boils and thickens. Season to taste with **ground nutmeg**.

Per serving: 585 calories, 27 g protein, 32 g carbohydrates, 39 g total fat, 171 mg cholesterol, 853 mg sodium

Garlic Veal Stew & Agnolotti

Preparation time: About 30 minutes

Cooking time: About 1¾ hours

The name means "fat little lambs," but *agnolotti* look more like plump semicircular ravioli. Typically filled with spinach and cheese, they were once difficult to find outside northern Italy, but now they're sold in the refrigerator case of most supermarkets. If you can't find fresh agnolotti, use fresh ravioli; either pasta is good with this pungent veal stew.

- 2 to 3 tablespoons olive oil or salad oil
- 2 pounds boneless veal shoulder, cut into 1½-inch cubes
- 1 large onion, finely chopped
- 12 cloves garlic, halved
- 1½ pounds pear-shaped (Roma-type) tomatoes, peeled, seeded, and chopped
- 1 cup tomato juice
- ½ cup dry white wine
- ⅓ cup small ripe olives
- 1 or 2 small dried hot red chiles
- 2 packages (9 oz. *each*) fresh agnolotti or ravioli
  Salt and pepper

Heat 2 tablespoons of the oil in a heavy 3- to 4-quart pan over medium-high heat. Add about half the veal and brown on all sides; remove meat from pan as it is browned. Repeat to brown remaining veal. Set all veal aside. Then add onion and about 1 tablespoon more oil (if needed) to pan; cook, stirring often, until onion is soft and lightly browned (6 to 8 minutes). Stir in garlic, tomatoes, tomato juice, wine, olives, and chiles.

Return meat to pan. Bring to a boil; then reduce heat, cover, and simmer until meat is tender when pierced (about 1 hour). Uncover and continue to cook, adjusting heat so stew boils gently, until sauce is thickened (about 15 more minutes).

Shortly before stew is done, in a 6- to 8-quart pan, cook agnolotti in 4 quarts boiling water just until tender to bite (5 to 6 minutes); or cook according to package directions.

While agnolotti are cooking, discard chiles from stew; skim and discard fat. Season to taste with salt and pepper. Drain agnolotti well; transfer to a warm rimmed platter. Spoon stew over agnolotti. Makes 6 servings.

Per serving: 519 calories, 46 g protein, 36 g carbohydrates, 21 g total fat, 197 mg cholesterol, 766 mg sodium

Pasta & Sausage in Madeira Cream

Preparation time: About 15 minutes

Cooking time: About 25 minutes

Madeira or sherry mellows the flavor of Italian sausage, helping the spicy meat blend smoothly with a mushroom cream sauce. Serve the rich mixture over spinach pasta.

- 1 pound mild Italian sausages, casings removed
- 12 ounces dry bite-size spinach pasta twists or spirals, such as rotelle or fusilli
- 4 ounces mushrooms, sliced
- 2 large cloves garlic, minced or pressed
- ¼ cup Madeira or dry sherry
- 1 cup whipping cream
- 1 teaspoon ground white pepper
- ¼ teaspoon ground nutmeg
- ½ to ¾ cup grated Parmesan cheese

Crumble sausages into a wide frying pan over medium-high heat; cook, stirring often, until well browned (10 to 15 minutes). Lift out sausage and set aside. Discard all but 2 tablespoons of the drippings.

In a 6- to 8-quart pan, cook pasta in 4 quarts boiling water just until tender to bite (about 10 minutes); or cook according to package directions.

Meanwhile, add mushrooms and garlic to drippings in frying pan; cook, stirring often, until mushrooms are brown (8 to 10 minutes). Add Madeira, stirring to scrape up browned bits from pan. Return sausage to pan; then add cream, white pepper, and nutmeg. Increase heat to high, bring to a boil, and boil until large, shiny bubbles form and sauce is slightly thickened (1 to 2 minutes).

Drain pasta and transfer to a warm serving bowl. Top with sausage sauce; mix lightly, using 2 forks. Serve with cheese to add to taste. Makes 4 to 6 servings.

Per serving: 717 calories, 29 g protein, 54 g carbohydrates, 43 g total fat, 180 mg cholesterol, 847 mg sodium

Italian Sausage & Pasta with Basil

Preparation time: About 15 minutes

Cooking time: About 20 minutes

The combination of robust sausages and green bell peppers at once recalls the boisterous bustle of an Italian street fair. To re-create that festive atmosphere any time, whip up this quick entrée: sautéed sausages, onions, peppers, and tomatoes, served over vermicelli and topped with cheese.

- 1 pound mild Italian sausages, casings removed
- 1 large onion, coarsely chopped
- 1 large green bell pepper (about 8 oz.), seeded and coarsely chopped
- 2 cloves garlic, minced or pressed
- 1 can (14½ oz. to 1 lb.) tomatoes
- 12 ounces dry vermicelli (not coil vermicelli) or spaghettini
- 2 to 3 tablespoons dry basil
- ¼ cup chopped parsley
- ¾ to 1 cup grated Parmesan cheese
- ¼ cup olive oil

Crumble sausages into a wide frying pan over medium-high heat. Cook, stirring often, until meat begins to brown. Add onion and bell pepper; continue to cook, stirring, until onion is soft but not brown (about 5 minutes). Spoon off and discard excess fat. Stir in garlic, then tomatoes (break up with a spoon) and their liquid. Bring to a boil; reduce heat and boil gently, uncovered, stirring often, until slightly thickened (about 10 minutes).

Meanwhile, in a 6- to 8-quart pan, cook vermicelli in 4 quarts boiling water just until tender to bite (8 to 10 minutes); or cook according to package directions. Drain well.

In a warm large serving bowl, combine basil, parsley, ½ cup of the cheese, and oil. Add vermicelli and mix lightly, using 2 forks. Top with sausage-tomato sauce. Serve with remaining ¼ to ½ cup cheese to add to taste. Makes 6 servings.

Per serving: 558 calories, 25 g protein, 52 g carbohydrates, 28 g total fat, 52 mg cholesterol, 848 mg sodium

Minced vegetables and tiny stelline make a savory
dressing for these Star-studded Baked Pork Chops (recipe
on facing page). Alongside, offer a room-temperature
stir-fry of multicolored bell pepper strips dressed
with olive oil, garlic, and herbs.

82

Pictured on facing page

Star-studded Baked Pork Chops

Preparation time: 15 to 20 minutes

Cooking time: About 20 minutes

Baking time: 25 to 30 minutes

To make a simplified version of stuffed pork chops, alternate browned chops with spoonfuls of pasta-vegetable dressing in a casserole, then bake.

½ cup (2½ to 3 oz.) dry tiny star-shaped pasta

1 egg

2 tablespoons butter or margarine

6 rib or loin pork chops (2 to 2½ lbs. *total*), about ¾ inch thick

1 cup *each* finely chopped celery and onion

1 clove garlic, minced or pressed

1 medium-size carrot (about 2 oz.), coarsely shredded

¼ cup chopped parsley

¾ teaspoon salt

½ teaspoon *each* pepper, dry sage leaves, and dry thyme leaves

In a 3-quart pan, cook pasta in 1½ quarts boiling water just until still slightly chewy (6 to 8 minutes); or cook a little less than time specified in package directions. Drain, rinse with cold water, and drain well again. In a medium-size bowl, beat egg; mix in pasta and set aside.

Melt butter in a wide frying pan over medium-high heat. Add pork chops and cook, turning once, just until browned on both sides (about 4 minutes *total*). Remove from pan and set aside. Reduce heat to medium and add celery, onion, garlic, and carrot; cook, stirring often, until vegetables are soft but not brown (6 to 8 minutes). Remove from heat and stir in parsley, salt, pepper, sage, and thyme. Then lightly stir vegetable mixture into pasta mixture.

Place a pork chop at one end of a greased 7- by 11-inch baking dish; spoon about a fifth of the pasta mixture over chop. Place another chop over pasta, overlapping it slightly. Continue alternating pasta and chops, ending with a pork chop. Spoon any remaining pasta mixture around chops. Cover and bake in a 350° oven just until chops are no longer pink in center; cut to test (25 to 30 minutes). Serve a portion of the pasta mixture with each chop. Makes 6 servings.

Per serving: 283 calories, 27 g protein, 13 g carbohydrates, 13 g total fat, 105 mg cholesterol, 396 mg sodium

Polish Sausage, Zucchini & Rigatoni

Preparation time: About 15 minutes

Cooking time: About 20 minutes

This hearty one-pan entrée combines chunky pasta, juicy sausages, and tender-crisp zucchini; fresh, peppery watercress provides a stylish final touch.

3 ounces (about 1 cup) dry rigatoni or elbow macaroni

3 tablespoons red wine vinegar

1 tablespoon *each* Dijon mustard and dry basil

12 ounces Polish sausage (kielbasa), cut into ¼-inch-thick slices

1 medium-size red onion, thinly sliced

3 small zucchini (about 8 oz. *total*), thinly sliced

1 bunch watercress (about 6 oz.), washed and crisped

In a wide frying pan, cook rigatoni in 1 inch boiling water just until tender to bite (10 to 15 minutes; or time according to package directions). Drain well and set aside.

While pasta is cooking, in a small bowl, stir together vinegar, mustard, and basil; set aside.

Rinse and dry pan; add sausage slices and stir over medium-high heat for 1 minute. Add onion and stir until softened (about 3 minutes). Add cooked pasta and vinegar mixture; stir until heated through (1 to 2 minutes). Stir in zucchini and cook just until tender-crisp to bite (about 3 minutes). Garnish in pan with bouquet of watercress and serve at once. Makes 4 servings.

Per serving: 384 calories, 17 g protein, 22 g carbohydrates, 25 g total fat, 60 mg cholesterol, 878 mg sodium

Rigatoni

It's an exceptional pasta dish that doesn't need some last-minute attention, but the two Italian recipes on this page finish baking entirely unattended. They're noteworthy in another respect, too: they feature the unusual combination of creamy pasta enclosed in tender-crisp puff pastry.

Tortellini Pasta Pie

2 packages (12 oz. *each*) frozen meat-filled tortellini
2 cups whipping cream
1 cup (about 5 oz.) grated Parmesan cheese
1 package (17¼ oz.) frozen puff pastry, thawed according to package directions
½ cup chopped parsley

In a 6- to 8-quart pan, cook tortellini in 4 quarts boiling water just until tender to bite (15 to 20 minutes); or cook according to package directions. Drain well. In a bowl, combine tortellini, cream, and cheese. Let stand until cool (or for up to 1 hour), stirring occasionally.

Meanwhile, on a lightly floured surface, separately roll out each sheet of pastry to make a 14-inch square. Ease one of the squares into a 9-inch spring-form pan, letting excess pastry drape over rim.

Stir parsley into tortellini mixture; pour mixture into pastry-lined pan. Top with second square of pastry. Trim excess pastry about ¼ inch from pan rim; set scraps aside. Pinch edges of pastry together and fold under, then crimp edge to seal. If desired, cut pastry scraps into decorative shapes, moisten undersides, and place atop pie. Slash top crust in about 6 places to allow steam to escape.

Creamy Pasta Pies

Bake on lowest rack of a 425° oven until pastry is richly browned (about 45 minutes). Let pie cool in pan on a rack for 15 minutes; then carefully remove pan sides. Let pie stand for at least 15 minutes (or up to 30 minutes); then cut into wedges to serve. Makes 6 to 8 servings.

Per serving: 840 calories, 26 g protein, 74 g carbohydrates, 49 g total fat, 142 mg cholesterol, 1,011 mg sodium

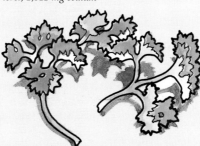

Venetian Pasta & Veal Pie

2 tablespoons butter or margarine
½ cup *each* chopped onion and carrots
8 ounces ground veal
4 ounces mushrooms, chopped
½ teaspoon dry thyme leaves
¼ cup dry white wine
¼ cup regular-strength chicken broth
2 tablespoons tomato paste
6 ounces dry slender pasta tubes, such as bucatini or perciatelli
1 cup frozen tiny peas
   Béchamel Sauce (recipe follows)
1 package (17¼ oz.) frozen puff pastry, thawed according to package directions

Melt butter in a wide frying pan over medium heat. Add onion and carrots; cook, stirring often, until onion is very soft (about 10 minutes). Crumble in veal and cook, stirring, until no longer pink. Stir in mushrooms, thyme, and wine. Reduce heat and simmer, uncovered, stirring often, until liquid has evaporated (about 15 minutes). Add broth and tomato paste; cook, stirring often, until thick (about 5 minutes). Let cool.

In a 5- to 6-quart pan, cook pasta in 3 quarts boiling water just until tender to bite (about 10 minutes); or cook according to package directions. Drain well.

In a bowl, combine meat mixture, pasta, and peas. Prepare Béchamel Sauce; stir warm sauce gently into pasta mixture.

Following directions given for Tortellini Pasta Pie (at left), roll out pastry, line spring-form pan, fill with pasta mixture, top with remaining pastry, finish edge, and decorate and slash top.

Bake on lowest rack of a 425° oven until pastry is richly browned (about 45 minutes). Let pie cool in pan on a rack for 15 minutes; then carefully remove pan sides. Let pie stand for at least 15 minutes (or up to 30 minutes); then cut into wedges to serve. Makes 6 to 8 servings.

Béchamel Sauce. Melt 3 tablespoons **butter** or margarine in a 1- to 1½-quart pan over medium heat. Blend in 3 tablespoons **all-purpose flour** and cook, stirring constantly, until bubbly. Remove from heat and gradually stir in ¾ cup *each* **regular-strength chicken broth** and **whipping cream**; return to heat and continue to cook, stirring, until sauce boils and thickens. Let cool slightly.

Per serving: 631 calories, 16 g protein, 53 g carbohydrates, 39 g total fat, 77 mg cholesterol, 672 mg sodium

Country-style Pappardelle

Preparation time: About 30 minutes

Baking time: 1¼ to 1½ hours

Cooking time: About 1 hour and 5 minutes

Italians prepare a richly flavored dish like this one with wild boar (*cinghiale*); we find country-style spareribs a reasonable (and more widely available!) substitute.

- 1 teaspoon dry rosemary
- ½ teaspoon coarsely ground pepper
- 3 cloves garlic, minced or pressed
- 3 tablespoons olive oil
- 2 to 2½ pounds country-style spareribs
- 1 medium-size red onion, thinly sliced
- 2 stalks celery, thinly sliced
- 1 medium-size carrot (about 2 oz.), finely chopped
- ¼ teaspoon whole cloves
- ½ cup dry red wine
- 1 can (6 oz.) tomato paste
- 1 can (14½ oz.) diced tomatoes
- 1 can (14½ oz.) regular-strength beef broth
- 2 packages (8½ oz. *each*) dry pappardelle (wide fettuccine), 1¼ pounds fresh pappardelle, or 1 pound dry extra-wide egg noodles
  Salt
- 1 to 2 tablespoons red wine vinegar
- ½ to ¾ cup grated Parmesan cheese

Mix rosemary, pepper, a third of the garlic, and 1 tablespoon of the oil. Coat spareribs with oil mixture on all sides. Place, fat side down, in a shallow baking pan. Bake, uncovered, in a 450° oven for 15 minutes; reduce oven temperature to 325° and continue to bake until meat is tender when pierced (1 to 1¼ more hours). Remove from oven and set aside.

Meanwhile, heat remaining 2 tablespoons oil in a 3½- to 4-quart pan over medium heat. Add onion, celery, and carrot; cook, stirring often, until onion is soft but not brown (6 to 8 minutes). Stir in remaining garlic, cloves, wine, tomato paste, tomatoes and their liquid, and 1½ cups of the broth. Bring to a boil; then reduce heat, cover, and simmer for 30 minutes. Uncover pan and adjust heat so mixture boils gently; cook, stirring occasionally, until thickened (about 20 minutes).

Remove spareribs from baking pan; pour off and discard fat from pan. Pour remaining ¼ cup broth into baking pan and stir to loosen browned drippings; add mixture to tomato-vegetable sauce.

Pull sparerib meat from bones in bite-size shreds; discard bones and fat. Stir shredded meat into sauce. (At this point, you may cover and refrigerate for up to 1 day.)

In an 8- to 10-quart pan, cook pasta in 5 quarts boiling water just until tender to bite (3 to 4 minutes for dry pappardelle, about 2 minutes for fresh pappardelle, 4 to 6 minutes for noodles); or cook according to package directions. Drain well.

While pasta is cooking, reheat sauce, if necessary. Season to taste with salt and vinegar. Place pasta in a large, wide serving bowl; add sauce. Mix lightly, using 2 spoons. Serve with cheese to add to taste. Makes 6 to 8 servings.

Per serving: 604 calories, 25 g protein, 60 g carbohydrates, 29 g total fat, 120 mg cholesterol, 688 mg sodium

Straw & Hay Pasta

Preparation time: About 5 minutes

Cooking time: 10 to 12 minutes

"Straw" and "hay"—golden and green pastas—are a classic duo. In this interpretation of the traditional dish, the sauce is a little lighter than you might expect.

- 8 ounces dry yellow and green tagliarini or 4½ ounces (half of a 9-oz. package) *each* fresh yellow and green linguine
- 1¼ cups half-and-half
- ⅓ to ½ cup julienne strips of thinly sliced cooked ham
- ⅓ cup frozen tiny peas
- ⅔ to ¾ cup grated Parmesan cheese

In a 5- to 6-quart pan, cook pasta in 3 quarts boiling water just until tender to bite (6 to 7 minutes for dry pasta, 1 to 2 minutes for fresh); or cook according to package directions.

Meanwhile, in a wide frying pan, combine half-and-half, ham, and peas; stir over medium heat until steaming (do not boil). Reduce heat to low. Drain pasta well and add to half-and-half mixture. Mix lightly, using 2 forks, until pasta has absorbed most of the liquid (2 to 3 minutes). Sprinkle with ⅓ cup of the cheese; mix lightly. Serve with remaining cheese to add to taste. Makes 4 servings.

Per serving: 407 calories, 19 g protein, 47 g carbohydrates, 16 g total fat, 73 mg cholesterol, 515 mg sodium

Mostaccioli & Swiss Cheese Casserole

Preparation time: 10 to 15 minutes

Cooking time: About 20 minutes

Baking time: About 30 minutes

In this new version of macaroni and cheese, *mostaccioli*—a pasta named for its fancied resemblance to little mustaches—mingles with Swiss cheese, spinach, and slivered ham in a mustardy sauce.

- 8 ounces dry mostaccioli or other small tube-shape pasta, such as penne
- ¼ cup butter or margarine
- ¼ cup all-purpose flour
- 2 cups milk
- ¼ teaspoon liquid hot pepper seasoning
- 1 tablespoon Dijon mustard
- 3 cups (12 oz.) shredded Swiss cheese
- 8 ounces cooked ham, cut into thin bite-size slivers
- 1 package (10 oz.) frozen chopped spinach, thawed

  Salt and pepper

In a 5- to 6-quart pan, cook mostaccioli in 3 quarts boiling water just until tender to bite (10 to 12 minutes); or cook according to package directions. Drain, rinse, and drain well again; set aside.

Melt butter in same pan over medium heat; stir in flour and cook, stirring, until bubbly. Remove from heat and gradually blend in milk. Increase heat to medium-high and cook, stirring constantly, until sauce comes to a boil. Add hot pepper seasoning, mustard, and 2 cups of the cheese; stir until cheese is melted. Remove from heat.

Add mostaccioli and ham to sauce; mix gently. Squeeze as much liquid as possible from spinach; then stir spinach into mostaccioli mixture. Spread in a shallow 2-quart casserole, then cover and bake in a 350° oven for 20 minutes. Uncover, sprinkle with remaining 1 cup cheese, and continue to bake until cheese is melted and mixture is bubbly (about 10 more minutes). Season to taste with salt and pepper. Makes 6 servings.

Per serving: 571 calories, 34 g protein, 40 g carbohydrates, 30 g total fat, 107 mg cholesterol, 949 mg sodium

---

Pictured on facing page

Linguine with Prosciutto & Olives

Preparation time: About 15 minutes

Cooking time: 8 to 10 minutes

The fragrance and sweet-salty flavor of premium-priced prosciutto permeate this dish—yet you need just 2 ounces of the meat to serve four. Cut into thin strips, the prosciutto mingles with stuffed olives, ribbons of linguine, and bright cherry tomatoes.

- 8 ounces dry linguine or 1 package (9 oz.) fresh linguine
- ¼ cup olive oil
- 2 ounces thinly sliced prosciutto, cut into ¼-inch-wide strips
- ½ cup thinly sliced green onions (including tops)
- 1 jar (3 oz.) pimento-stuffed olives, drained
- 1 cup cherry tomatoes, cut into halves
- ½ to ⅔ cup grated Parmesan cheese

In a 5- to 6-quart pan, cook linguine in 3 quarts boiling water just until tender to bite (8 to 10 minutes for dry pasta, 1 to 2 minutes for fresh); or cook according to package directions. Drain well and transfer to a warm serving bowl.

While linguine is cooking, heat oil in a medium-size frying pan over medium-high heat; add prosciutto and cook, stirring often, until lightly browned (3 to 4 minutes). Add onions and stir just until they begin to soften. Add olives and tomatoes; shake pan often until olives are hot (about 2 minutes). Pour prosciutto mixture over linguine; mix lightly, using 2 forks. Serve with cheese to add to taste. Makes 4 servings.

Per serving: 444 calories, 16 g protein, 45 g carbohydrates, 22 g total fat, 18 mg cholesterol, 1,059 mg sodium

■ *To Microwave:* Cook linguine as directed above. Meanwhile, arrange prosciutto strips in a 2-quart microwave-safe casserole. Microwave, covered, on **HIGH (100%)** for 2 to 2½ minutes or until prosciutto is lightly browned, stirring once. Stir in oil and onions. Microwave, covered, on **HIGH (100%)** for 2 to 3 minutes or until oil is hot and onions begin to soften. Lightly mix in olives and tomatoes. Microwave, covered, on **HIGH (100%)** for 1 to 2 minutes or until heated through. Let stand, covered, while draining linguine. Add linguine to prosciutto mixture; mix lightly, using 2 forks. Serve with cheese to add to taste.

*For the speediest of main dishes, toss together
vivid Linguine with Prosciutto & Olives (recipe on facing
page), then serve with country-style Italian bread and a
salad of cooked vegetables in a vinaigrette dressing.*

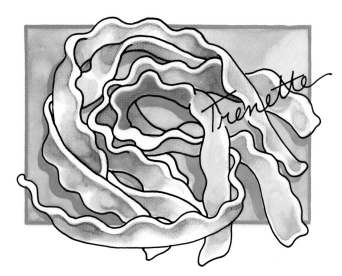
Trenette

Bacon & Egg Carbonara

Preparation time: About 10 minutes

Cooking time: About 10 minutes

Those reliable staples, bacon and eggs, are supported by a thin pasta such as capellini or vermicelli to make an irresistible entrée for a casual supper.

    8   ounces sliced bacon (about 10 slices), cut
        into 1-inch squares
    8   ounces dry thin pasta such as capellini or
        vermicelli; or 1 package (9 oz.) fresh angel
        hair pasta
    2   cups sour cream
    ¼   cup chopped chives or thinly sliced green
        onions (including tops)
    4   egg yolks
    1   cup (about 5 oz.) grated Parmesan cheese

In a wide frying pan, cook bacon over medium heat until crisp. Spoon off and discard all but 3 tablespoons of the drippings; keep pan with bacon warm over lowest heat.

In a 5- to 6-quart pan, cook pasta in 3 quarts boiling water just until tender to bite (about 3 minutes for dry capellini, 8 to 10 minutes for dry vermicelli, 1 to 2 minutes for fresh angel hair pasta); or cook according to package directions. After adding pasta to boiling water, spoon ½ cup of the sour cream into each of 4 wide, shallow bowls; place bowls in a 200° oven while completing cooking.

Drain pasta well; add pasta and chives to bacon in pan. Mix lightly, using 2 forks. Spoon an equal portion of pasta mixture into each warm bowl. Make a nest in center of each; slip in an egg yolk. Mix each portion individually and sprinkle with cheese. Makes 4 servings.

Per serving: 839 calories, 33 g protein, 50 g carbohydrates, 56 g total fat, 312 mg cholesterol, 1,031 mg sodium

Baked Trenette with Prosciutto & Radicchio

Preparation time: About 15 minutes

Cooking time: About 20 minutes

Baking time: About 20 minutes

Trenette (*trinette*) are long, flat, medium-wide noodles, sometimes ruffle-edged in their dry form. Fresh trenette is the first choice to serve with pesto on its home ground of Liguria. In this recipe, though, we use the dried pasta, baking it with slivered radicchio in a creamy-rich cheese sauce.

    8   ounces dry trenette or dry fettuccine
    3   tablespoons butter or margarine
    2   small heads radicchio (6 to 8 oz. *total*), cored
        and coarsely slivered
    4   ounces sliced prosciutto, cut into strips
    1½ cups whipping cream
    ¼   teaspoon *each* ground nutmeg and ground
        white pepper
    ⅓   cup dry white wine
    1½ cups (6 oz.) shredded fontina cheese
    ¾   cup grated Parmesan cheese

In a 5- to 6-quart pan, cook trenette in 3 quarts boiling water just until tender to bite (8 to 10 minutes); or cook according to package directions. Drain well; transfer to a greased shallow 2-quart baking dish.

While trenette is cooking, melt butter in a wide frying pan over medium heat. Add radicchio and prosciutto; cook, stirring constantly, until radicchio is wilted and prosciutto begins to brown.

Lift radicchio mixture from pan, add to trenette in baking dish, and mix lightly. Then add cream, nutmeg, white pepper, and wine to pan. Increase heat to high and bring to a boil; boil, stirring often, until reduced to 1¼ cups. Remove from heat and add fontina cheese; stir over medium heat until cheese is melted. Mix in ½ cup of the Parmesan cheese, then pour sauce over trenette mixture. Sprinkle with remaining ¼ cup Parmesan cheese.

Bake, uncovered, in a 400° oven until heated through (about 20 minutes). Makes 4 servings.

Per serving: 854 calories, 34 g protein, 47 g carbohydrates, 59 g total fat, 254 mg cholesterol, 1,027 mg sodium

Super-rich Fettuccine

Preparation time: About 5 minutes

Cooking time: 8 to 10 minutes

This luscious dish combines two classics—fettuccine Alfredo and pasta carbonara—with sublime results.

  6 slices bacon (about 5 oz.)
  ½ cup (¼ lb.) unsalted butter or margarine
  3 cloves garlic, minced or pressed
  1 egg
  1 cup whipping cream
  1 cup (about 5 oz.) grated Parmesan cheese
  ¼ teaspoon dry oregano leaves
12 ounces fresh fettuccine or 10 ounces dry fettuccine
  3 tablespoons minced parsley
     Salt and pepper

In a wide frying pan, cook bacon over medium heat until crisp. Lift out, drain, crumble, and set aside; discard drippings. Melt butter in pan; add garlic and cook, stirring often, until garlic turns opaque (1 to 2 minutes). Remove from heat and add bacon.

In a small bowl, beat egg with cream, cheese, and oregano. Add egg mixture to bacon mixture and stir over medium heat until sauce is slightly thickened.

Meanwhile, in a 6- to 8-quart pan, cook fettuccine in 4 quarts boiling water just until tender to bite (3 to 4 minutes for fresh pasta, 8 to 10 minutes for dry); or cook according to package directions. Drain well and transfer to a warm serving bowl.

Add sauce and parsley to pasta; mix lightly, using 2 forks, until pasta is well coated. Season to taste with salt and pepper. Makes 4 to 6 servings.

Per serving: 691 calories, 25 g protein, 41 g carbohydrates, 48 g total fat, 254 mg cholesterol, 700 mg sodium

Stovetop Moussaka with Green Fettuccine

Preparation time: About 25 minutes

Draining time: 30 minutes to 1 hour

Cooking time: About 45 minutes

Moussaka is usually baked, but there's a faster way to cook this favorite lamb and eggplant dish—combine the familiar elements in a wide frying pan over direct heat. Before serving, spoon hot pasta around the edges of the skillet to share the cooking juices.

    1 large eggplant (about 2 lbs.), unpeeled, cut into 1-inch cubes
 1½ teaspoons salt
    2 tablespoons olive oil
    1 pound lean ground lamb
    1 medium-size onion, finely chopped
    2 cloves garlic, minced or pressed
    4 large pear-shaped (Roma-type) tomatoes (about 12 oz. *total*), peeled, seeded, and chopped
    1 can (8 oz.) tomato sauce
    3 tablespoons minced parsley
 1½ teaspoons cumin seeds
    1 teaspoon crushed dried hot red chiles
    8 ounces dry green fettuccine or 1 package (9 oz.) fresh green fettuccine
    1 package (10 oz.) frozen pearl onions, thawed
   ½ to 1 cup plain yogurt or sour cream

Mix eggplant with salt; transfer to a colander and let drain for 30 minutes to 1 hour. Rinse with cold water, drain, and pat dry.

Heat oil in a wide frying pan over medium-high heat. Add eggplant and cook, turning often with a wide spatula, until lightly browned (6 to 8 minutes). Add 2 tablespoons water; stir and turn eggplant, then quickly cover pan. At 1-minute intervals, add 2 tablespoons more water, turning eggplant and covering again after each addition; cook until eggplant is very soft when pressed (about 6 minutes *total*). Transfer to a bowl and set aside.

Crumble lamb into pan and stir in chopped onion. Increase heat to high and cook, stirring often, until meat is very well browned (about 8 minutes). Stir in garlic; then stir in eggplant and any accumulated juices, tomatoes, tomato sauce, parsley, cumin seeds, and chiles. Reduce heat to medium, cover, and boil gently until tomatoes are very soft (about 20 minutes).

Meanwhile, in a 5- to 6-quart pan, cook fettuccine in 3 quarts boiling water just until tender to bite (8 to 10 minutes for dry pasta, 3 to 4 minutes for fresh); or cook according to package directions. Drain well.

When lamb mixture is done, add pearl onions and gently stir until heated through (1 to 2 minutes). Gently push lamb mixture to one side or to center of pan; add fettuccine next to or around lamb. Serve with yogurt to add to taste. Makes 6 servings.

Per serving: 473 calories, 23 g protein, 42 g carbohydrates, 25 g total fat, 105 mg cholesterol, 526 mg sodium

First oven-browned, then simmered to tenderness
in a rich red sauce, succulent lamb ribs make a hearty
meal for a chilly day. If you can't find the distinctive
pasta called rustici, just substitute bow ties (farfalle);
Rustic Lamb Spareribs with Eggplant Sauce (recipe
on facing page) are delicious either way.

Rustic Lamb Spareribs with Eggplant Sauce

Preparation time: *About 15 minutes*

Cooking time: *About 1¾ hours*

Baking time: *30 to 40 minutes*

Rustici, an unusual dry pasta with a homemade look, complements this dish of tender lamb spareribs in a spicy, eggplant-thickened tomato sauce.

> 2 tablespoons olive oil
> 1 small eggplant (8 to 10 oz.), unpeeled, diced
> 4 cloves garlic, minced or pressed
> 1 can (14½ oz.) pear-shaped tomatoes
> 1 large can (15 oz.) tomato sauce
> ½ cup port wine
> 1 tablespoon firmly packed brown sugar
> 1½ teaspoons dry oregano leaves
> 1 dry bay leaf
> 1 cinnamon stick (about 3 inches long)
> ⅓ cup chopped parsley
> Salt and pepper
> 2 to 2½ pounds lamb spareribs
> ⅓ cup water
> 8 ounces dry rustici or bow-shaped pasta

Heat oil in a 3- to 4-quart pan over medium-high heat. Add eggplant and cook, stirring often, until eggplant is very soft (8 to 10 minutes). Stir in garlic, tomatoes (break up with a spoon) and their liquid, tomato sauce, port, sugar, oregano, bay leaf, cinnamon stick, and all but 1 tablespoon of the parsley. Bring to a boil; then reduce heat, partially cover, and simmer until very thick (about 30 minutes). Season to taste with salt and pepper.

Meanwhile, arrange lamb spareribs, fat side up, in a single layer in a shallow baking pan. Bake, uncovered, in a 450° oven until well browned (30 to 40 minutes). Lift lamb from baking pan, cut between bones to separate, and transfer to pan with tomato-eggplant sauce.

Pour off and discard fat in baking pan. Then pour in ⅓ cup water, stirring to dissolve browned bits. Add water mixture to ribs in sauce; cover and simmer over low heat until lamb is very tender when pierced (about 1 hour). Skim and discard fat from sauce.

When lamb is almost tender, in a 5- to 6-quart pan, cook rustici in 3 quarts boiling water just until tender to bite (10 to 12 minutes); or cook according to package directions. Drain well and transfer to a warm deep platter; spoon sauce and ribs over pasta. Sprinkle with remaining 1 tablespoon parsley. Makes 4 servings.

Per serving: 720 calories, 37 g protein, 66 g carbohydrates, 34 g total fat, 163 mg cholesterol, 901 mg sodium

Lamb & Orzo, Mediterranean Style

Preparation time: *About 10 minutes*

Cooking time: *About 25 minutes*

A crisp green salad and a warm loaf of crusty bread are superb, simple accompaniments for this one-pan meal of ground lamb and rice-shaped pasta.

> ½ teaspoon salt
> 1 pound lean ground lamb
> 1 large onion, finely chopped
> 2 cloves garlic, minced or pressed
> 1 can (14½ oz. to 1 lb.) tomatoes
> 1 chicken bouillon cube
> 1½ cups hot water
> ½ teaspoon dry oregano leaves
> ¼ teaspoon pepper
> 1 cup (about 8 oz.) dry rice-shaped pasta
> 1 package (10 oz.) frozen chopped spinach, thawed
> ½ to ¾ cup grated Parmesan cheese

Sprinkle salt into a wide frying pan over medium-high heat. Crumble lamb into pan and cook, stirring often, until meat begins to brown (3 to 5 minutes). Reduce heat to medium, stir in onion, and continue to cook, stirring, until onion is soft but not brown (about 5 minutes). Spoon off and discard excess fat. Add garlic, tomatoes (break up with a spoon) and their liquid, bouillon cube, water, oregano, and pepper. Bring mixture to a boil, stirring to dissolve bouillon cube; then stir in pasta. Reduce heat, cover, and boil gently, stirring once or twice, until pasta is just tender to bite (10 to 12 minutes; or time according to package directions).

Meanwhile, squeeze as much liquid as possible from spinach. Stir spinach into pasta mixture just until heated through. Serve with cheese to add to taste. Makes 4 servings.

Per serving: 644 calories, 35 g protein, 54 g carbohydrates, 32 g total fat, 93 mg cholesterol, 1,046 mg sodium

Risotto: Italian Rice

Risotto, Italy's celebrated creamy rice, resembles pasta in a couple of ways: it's usually served as the course preceding the main dish, and it can accommodate a seemingly infinite variety of seasonings and added ingredients. Try it in its basic form, or savor it dressed up with vegetables, herbs, and mushrooms. Plain or fancy, it's good served before or alongside roasted or grilled meats or poultry.

Risotto enjoys its greatest popularity in northern Italy (rice is grown in the valley of the Po River), where it turns up in regional versions from the Adriatic to the Mediterranean coasts; saffron-hued *risotto alla milanese* is a deserved classic.

The recipes presented here can be made with short-grain rice (such as pearl) or with medium-grain rice, including Italian arborio. Because risotto simmers uncovered, the flavor of the cooking liquid will be concentrated—so if you use salted canned broth, dilute it with water so the finished risotto won't be too salty.

Basic Risotto

- 3 tablespoons butter or margarine
- 1 medium-size onion, finely chopped
- 1 cup short- or medium-grain white rice
- 1¾ cups regular-strength chicken or beef broth
- 1¼ to 1¾ cups water
- ¼ to ½ cup grated Parmesan cheese

Melt butter in an 10- to 12-inch frying pan over medium heat. Add onion and cook, stirring, until onion is translucent (about 5 minutes). Add rice and stir until opaque (about 2 minutes). Add broth and water (use 1¼ cups water for short-grain rice, 1½ cups water for medium-grain rice).

Increase heat to high and bring to a boil. Reduce heat and boil very gently, uncovered, just until rice is tender to bite (20 to 25 minutes); stir occasionally at first, then more frequently as liquid is almost absorbed. Add more broth or water, ¼ cup at a time, if needed to prevent sticking.

Just before serving, stir in cheese to taste. Makes about 5 servings.

Per serving: 251 calories, 6 g protein, 34 g carbohydrates, 10 g total fat, 23 mg cholesterol, 550 mg sodium

Porcini Mushroom Risotto

- 1 ounce dried porcini mushrooms (cèpes)
- 1½ cups hot water
- 1¾ cups regular-strength chicken or beef broth
- 3 tablespoons butter or margarine
- 1 tablespoon olive oil
- 1 medium-size onion, finely chopped
- 1 clove garlic, minced or pressed
- 1 cup short- or medium-grain white rice
- ¾ to 1 cup grated Parmesan cheese

Place mushrooms in a bowl, add hot water, and let stand until mushrooms are soft (20 to 30 minutes). Lift out mushrooms (reserve soaking liquid) and rinse well, using your fingers to work out any grit; squeeze mushrooms gently to remove excess liquid. Chop mushrooms coarsely; set aside.

Pour soaking liquid through a fine strainer (do not disturb sediment on bottom of bowl) into a 1-quart measuring cup. Add broth; if necessary, add water to make 3 cups total.

Melt butter in oil in an 10- to 12-inch frying pan over medium heat. Add onion and cook, stirring, until onion is translucent (about 5 minutes). Then add garlic and rice; stir until rice is opaque (about 2 minutes). Add mushrooms and soaking liquid–broth mixture, then continue cooking as directed for Basic Risotto (at left).

Just before serving, stir in ¼ to ½ cup of the cheese; serve with remaining cheese to add to taste. Makes about 5 servings.

Per serving: 311 calories, 9 g protein, 38 g carbohydrates, 14 g total fat, 29 mg cholesterol, 313 mg sodium

Radicchio or Endive Risotto

Pictured on page 95

- 1 tablespoon olive oil
- 3 cups shredded radicchio (about 6 oz.) or Belgian endive (about 12 oz.)
- 1 tablespoon lemon juice (omit if using endive)
  Basic Risotto (at left)
- 1 small clove garlic, minced or pressed
- 1 tablespoon butter or margarine
  Whole radicchio or Belgian endive leaves, washed and crisped
  Lemon wedges
  Italian (flat-leaf) parsley sprigs

Heat oil in a 3- to 4-quart pan over high heat. Add shredded radicchio and lemon juice; stir just until radicchio is wilted (about 2 minutes). Lift out and set aside.

In same pan, prepare Basic Risotto, adding garlic with rice; when you add cheese, gently stir in cooked radicchio and the 1 tablespoon butter. Serve in a warm bowl lined with radicchio leaves; or place leaves on individual plates and spoon risotto into leaves. Garnish with lemon wedges and parsley sprigs. Makes 4 to 6 servings.

Per serving: 302 calories, 7 g protein, 36 g carbohydrates, 15 g total fat, 30 mg cholesterol, 576 mg sodium

Green Risotto with Sautéed Liver

2 medium-size leeks (about 8 oz. *total*)
5 tablespoons butter or margarine
½ cup finely chopped parsley
2 teaspoons dry basil
1 cup short- or medium-grain white rice
1¾ cups regular-strength chicken or beef broth
1¼ to 1¾ cups water
1 pound chicken livers, drained and cut into halves; or 1 pound calf's liver, cut into ¼-inch-wide bite-size strips
2 tablespoons dry sherry
¼ to ½ cup grated Parmesan cheese Parsley sprigs

Trim and discard roots and tough parts of green tops from leeks; cut leeks in half lengthwise, rinse well, and slice thinly crosswise.

Melt 3 tablespoons of the butter in a 12- to 14-inch frying pan over medium heat. Add leeks, chopped parsley, and basil. Cook, stirring, until

leeks are tender to bite (about 5 minutes). Add rice and stir until opaque (about 2 minutes); add broth and water and continue cooking as directed for Basic Risotto (facing page).

Meanwhile, melt remaining 2 tablespoons butter in a wide frying pan over high heat. Add half the livers. Cook, turning, until browned on outside but still pink in center; cut to test (1 to 2 minutes). Remove to a warm bowl and keep warm while cooking remaining livers. Return all livers to pan, add sherry, and stir gently just until heated through.

To serve, stir cheese into risotto. Then top risotto with livers; garnish with parsley sprigs. Makes 4 servings.

Per serving: 527 calories, 29 g protein, 51 g carbohydrates, 23 g total fat, 544 mg cholesterol, 859 mg sodium

Pan-grilled Risotto with Mozzarella & Basil

Basic Risotto (facing page)
1 clove garlic, minced or pressed
8 ounces mozzarella cheese, diced
2 tablespoons minced fresh basil leaves or 2 teaspoons dry basil
¾ to 1 cup grated Parmesan cheese About ¼ cup butter or margarine

Prepare Basic Risotto, but add garlic with rice and omit Parmesan cheese called for.

When risotto is done, remove from heat and let cool for 25 to 30 minutes. Then stir in mozzarella cheese, basil, and ½ cup of the Parmesan cheese. Line a 9- by 13-inch pan with foil. Spread risotto evenly in foil-lined pan. Cover and refrigerate until firm (at least 2 hours) or for up to 3 days.

Invert risotto onto a board; carefully peel off and discard foil. Cut risotto into 3-inch squares, then cut each square diagonally in half.

Melt 1 tablespoon of the butter in a wide nonstick frying pan over medium-high heat. Add several risotto triangles (do not crowd pan); cook, turning once, until golden brown on both sides (5 to 6 minutes *total*). As triangles are cooked, arrange them in a single layer on a heatproof platter and keep warm in a 300° oven. Cook remaining triangles, adding remaining butter as needed.

Serve hot, with remaining ¼ to ½ cup Parmesan cheese to add to taste. Makes about 6 servings.

Per serving: 416 calories, 15 g protein, 30 g carbohydrates, 26 g total fat, 75 mg cholesterol, 802 mg sodium

Index

Agnolotti, garlic veal stew &, 80
Angel hair
  primavera, 32
  with shrimp & mint butter sauce, 52
Antipasto pasta salad, 22
Artichoke hearts, cooked, 22
Asparagus
  linguine with morels &, 34
  & scallops, stir-fried, on cool pasta, 21

Bacon & egg carbonara, 88
Baked chicken, tomato-cheese pasta with, 55
Baked polenta
  saucy chicken &, 69
  & sausages, 69
Baked pork chops, star-studded, 83
Baked tomato spaghetti, 30
Baked trenette with prosciutto & radicchio, 88
Barbecued crab with spaghetti, 50
Barbecued quail with pappardelle in mushroom sauce, 73
Barbecue sauce, beef-mushroom spaghetti in, 77
Basic risotto, 92
Basil
  -cilantro pesto, 33
  Italian sausage & pasta with, 81
  mignonette, penne with tomato &, 24
  mignonette dressing, 24
  mozzarella &, pan-grilled risotto with, 93
  sauce, lime-, spaghetti squash with, 45
Bean
  pinto, & pasta soup, 16
  red, & lamb soup, 16
  salad, broccoli, pasta &, 25
  white, pasta & sausage soup, 14
Béchamel sauce, 84
Beef
  braciola & meatballs with fusilli, 75
  lasagne with spinach, 77
  -mushroom spaghetti in barbecue sauce, 77
  spicy Mediterranean meatballs, 78
  wine-braised chuck roast with bow ties, 76
Bell pepper pasta, red, 6
Bow ties, wine-braised chuck roast with, 76
Braciola & meatballs with fusilli, 75
Brandied shrimp, tricolor pasta with, 52
Broccoli
  cream sauce, capellini with, 37
  pasta & bean salad, 25
Broth, fresh pea & pasta, 13
Bucatini, Amatrice style, 29
Butter sauce
  mint, angel hair with shrimp &, 52
  pine nut–, 6

Cabbage
  soup, ravioli &, 11
  toasted, with noodles, 42
Cakes, gorgonzola polenta, 68
Calamari, fettuccine with, 49
Cannelloni, shiitake & cheese, 60
Capellini with broccoli cream sauce, 37
Carbonara, bacon & egg, 88
Carbonara, chicken, 65
Carbonara, tuna, 48
Casserole, mostaccioli & Swiss cheese, 86
Cauliflower sauce, seashells with, 28

Chard, Swiss, pasta with, 34
Chard stuffing, orzo &, 56
Cheese
  cannelloni, shiitake &, 60
  fettuccine Emmenthaler, 36
  filling, chile-, 65
  pasta, tomato-, with baked chicken, 55
  sauce, mushroom-, tortellini with, 36
  sauce, tomato-, wide noodles in, 30
  Swiss, mostaccioli &, casserole, 86
  tart, polenta, 68
  vegetables &, 27–45
Chèvre & olives, tagliarini with, 41
Chicken
  baked, tomato-cheese pasta with, 55
  carbonara, 65
  chili sauce, spaghetti with, 57
  crisp won ton salad, 20
  fettuccine verde with, 64
  grilled, & pasta primavera salad, 19
  grilled, farfalle with, & pesto cream, 64
  lasagne, Mexican, 65
  livers with garlic pasta, 67
  mustard, rooster crests with, 57
  & noodles with pimentos, 58
  -noodle yogurt soup, 12
  orzo-stuffed roast, & vegetables, 56
  oven, & linguine, 58
  pasta &, with sweet-sour tomato sauce, 63
  in port cream with fettuccine, 63
  & prosciutto filling, 61
  saucy, & baked polenta, 69
  tortellini soup, 12
Chicken liver(s)
  with garlic pasta, 67
  green risotto with sautéed liver, 93
Chile
  -cheese filling, 65
  dressing, 21
Chili sauce, chicken, spaghetti with, 57
Chuck roast, wine-braised, with bow ties, 76
Cilantro
  pesto, 33
  pesto, basil-, 33
Classic pesto, 33
Colorful flavored pastas, 6
Cooked artichoke hearts, 22
Cool pasta, stir-fried asparagus & scallops on, 21
Country-style pappardelle, 85
Crab, barbecued, with spaghetti, 50
Cream
  Madeira, pasta & sausage in, 81
  pesto, farfalle with grilled chicken &, 64
  port, chicken in, with fettuccine, 63
  sauce, 61, 80
  sauce, capellini with broccoli, 37
  tomato, straw & hay in, 29
Creamy pasta pies, 84
Crisp won ton salad, 20
Crisp won ton strips, 20

Dill spaghetti squash, onion-, 45
Double mushroom sauce, linguine with, 36
Dressings
  basil mignonette, 24
  chile, 21
  pesto, 22
  raspberry vinaigrette, 22
  sesame-lemon, 21
  sesame seed, 25
Dried tomato pesto, 33

Egg
  carbonara, bacon &, 88
  pasta, 8

Eggplant sauce, rustic lamb spareribs with, 91
Emmenthaler (cheese), fettuccine, 36
Endive risotto, radicchio or, 92

Farfalle with grilled chicken & pesto cream, 64
Fettuccine
  with calamari, 49
  chicken in port cream with, 63
  Emmenthaler, 36
  green, stovetop moussaka with, 89
  spinach, parsley pesto grilled vegetables &, 27
  super-rich, 89
  verde with chicken, 64
Food processor pasta, 8
Fresh herb pasta, 6
Fresh pea & pasta broth, 13
Fresh tuna puttanesca, 48
Fusilli, braciola & meatballs with, 75

Garbanzo pasta, 40
Garlic
  orecchiette with spinach &, 39
  pasta, chicken livers with, 67
  veal stew & agnolotti, 80
Ginger linguine with smoked scallops, 53
Gjetost sauce, Norwegian meatballs with, 78
Gorgonzola polenta cakes, 68
Green fettuccine, stovetop moussaka with, 89
Green lasagne Donatello, 80
Green minestrone, winter, 13
Green noodles, scallops &, 53
Green risotto with sautéed liver, 93
Grilled chicken & pasta primavera salad, 19
Grilled chicken & pesto cream, farfalle with, 64
Grilled swordfish with stir-fried noodles, 49
Grilled vegetables, parsley pesto, & spinach fettuccine, 27

Herb
  pasta, fresh, 6
  pesto, spinach-, 33
Herbed meatballs, 78
Homemade egg pasta, 8–9
Hoppin' John soup, 17
Hot pasta & tuna salad, 21

Italian rice (risotto), 92–93
Italian sausage & pasta with basil, 81

Lamb
  & orzo, Mediterranean style, 91
  soup, red bean &, 16
  spareribs, rustic, with eggplant sauce, 91
  stovetop moussaka with green fettuccine, 89
Lasagne
  green, Donatello, 80
  Mexican chicken, 65
  packets, 37
  spaghetti squash, 44
  with spinach, 77
  vegetable, 39
Lemon dressing, sesame-, 21
Lime-basil sauce, spaghetti squash with, 45
Linguine
  with double mushroom sauce, 36
  ginger, with smoked scallops, 53
  with morels & asparagus, 34
  oven chicken &, 58
  with prosciutto & olives, 86
  with zucchini, 32
Liver(s)
  chicken, with garlic pasta, 67
  sautéed, green risotto with, 93

Madeira cream, pasta & sausage in, 81
Meatballs
  braciola &, with fusilli, 75
  herbed, 78
  Norwegian, with gjetost sauce, 78
  raisin, 76
  spicy Mediterranean, 78
Meats, 75–91. *See also* Beef; Lamb; Pork; Sausage(s); Veal
Mediterranean meatballs, spicy, 78
Mediterranean pasta soup, 17
Mexican chicken lasagne, 65
Microwave polenta, 69
Minestrone, winter green, 13
Mint butter sauce, angel hair with shrimp &, 52
Minted pesto butter, 64
Morels & asparagus, linguine with, 34
Mostaccioli & Swiss cheese casserole, 86
Moussaka, stovetop, with green fettuccine, 89
Mozzarella & basil, pan-grilled risotto with, 93
Mushroom
  -cheese sauce, tortellini with, 36
  risotto, porcini, 92
  sauce, double, linguine with, 36
  sauce, pappardelle in, barbecued quail with, 73
  shiitake & cheese cannelloni, 60
  spaghetti, beef-, in barbecue sauce, 77
  -tomato sauce, 61
Mustard chicken, rooster crests with, 57

Noodle(s)
  chicken &, with pimentos, 58
  green, scallops &, 53
  salad, sesame, 24
  stir-fried, grilled swordfish with, 49
  toasted cabbage with, 42
  wide, in tomato-cheese sauce, 30
  yogurt soup, chicken-, 12
Norwegian meatballs with gjetost sauce, 78
Nutritional data, how to interpret, 5

Olives
  chèvre &, tagliarini with, 41
  prosciutto &, linguine with, 86
Onion(s)
  -dill spaghetti squash, 45
  peppers &, pasta with, 40
  sauce, tomato-, 67
Oranges, tortellini &, turkey with, 70
Orecchiette with spinach & garlic, 39
Orzo
  & chard stuffing, 56
  lamb &, Mediterranean style, 91
  -stuffed roast chicken & vegetables, 56
Oven chicken & linguine, 58

Packets, lasagne, 37
Pan-grilled risotto with mozzarella & basil, 93
Pappardelle
  country-style, 85
  in mushroom sauce, barbecued quail with, 73
Parchment, seafood in, 50
Parmesan, turkey, spaghetti with, 67
Parsley pesto, 28
Parsley pesto grilled vegetables & spinach fettuccine, 27
Pasta
  & bean salad, broccoli, 25
  broth, fresh pea &, 13
  & chicken with sweet-sour tomato sauce, 63

(Continued on page 96)

*The most colorful member of the endive family
takes the spotlight in Radicchio Risotto (recipe on page
92). Sliver the purple-red radicchio leaves and blend them
with hot, creamy rice; then spoon the melange into cuplike
whole leaves for a handsome presentation. Complete
the meal with grilled Italian sausages.*

Sunset
Proof-of-Purchase
ISBN 0-376-02523-9

Pasta (cont'd)
  cooking basics, 4–5
  cool, stir-fried asparagus & scallops on, 21
  egg, 8
  food processor, 8
  fresh herb, 6
  garbanzo, 40
  garlic, chicken livers with, 67
  homemade, 6, 8–9
  Italian sausage &, with basil, 81
  pea pod & turkey, 72
  with peppers & onions, 40
  pies, creamy, 84
  pilaf, 42
  primavera salad, grilled chicken &, 19
  red, white & green, 41
  red bell pepper, 6
  salad, antipasto, 22
  salad, summertime, 25
  & sausage in Madeira cream, 81
  & sausage soup, white bean, 14
  soup, Mediterranean, 17
  soup, pinto bean &, 16
  spinach, 6
  straw & hay, 85
  tomato-cheese, with baked chicken, 55
  tricolor, with brandied shrimp, 52
  & tuna salad, hot, 21
  vegetables as, 44–45
Pea, fresh, & pasta broth, 13
Pea pod & turkey pasta, 72
Penne
  with smoked salmon, 47
  with tomato & basil mignonette, 24
Pepper(s)
  & onions, pasta with, 40
  pasta, red bell, 6
Perciatelli, turkey marinara with, 70
Pesto
  basil-cilantro, 33
  cilantro, 33
  classic, 33
  cream, farfalle with grilled chicken &, 64
  dressing, 22
  dried tomato, 33
  parsley, 28
  parsley, grilled vegetables & spinach fettuccine, 27
  pasta with, 33
  salad, tortellini, shrimp &, 22
  spinach-herb, 33
Pies
  tortellini pasta, 84
  Venetian pasta & veal, 84
Pilaf, pasta, 42
Pimentos, chicken & noodles with, 58
Pine nut–butter sauce, 6
Pinto bean & pasta soup, 16
Pistou soup with sausage, 14
Polenta
  baked, 69
  baked, & sausages, 69
  baked, saucy chicken &, 69
  cakes, gorgonzola, 68
  cheese tart, 68
  microwave, 69
  plain & fancy, 68–69
  stove-top, 68
Polish sausage, zucchini & rigatoni, 83
Porcini mushroom risotto, 92
Pork
  baked polenta & sausages, 69
  chops, star-studded baked, 83
  country-style pappardelle, 85
  Italian sausage & pasta with basil, 81
  pasta & sausage in Madeira cream, 81
  pistou soup with sausage, 14
  Polish sausage, zucchini & rigatoni, 83
  white bean, pasta & sausage soup, 14
Port cream, chicken in, with fettuccine, 63

Pot sticker tortellini, 61
Poultry, 55–73. See also Chicken; Quail; Turkey
Prosciutto
  filling, chicken &, 61
  & olives, linguine with, 86
  & radicchio, baked trenette with, 88

Quail, barbecued, with pappardelle in mushroom sauce, 73

Radicchio
  or endive risotto, 92
  prosciutto &, baked trenette with, 88
Raisin meatballs, 76
Raspberry vinaigrette, 22
Ravioli
  & cabbage soup, 11
  won ton, 60
Red, white & green pasta, 41
Red bean & lamb soup, 16
Red bell pepper pasta, 6
Rigatoni, Polish sausage, zucchini &, 83
Risotto, 92–93
  basic, 92
  green, with sautéed liver, 93
  pan-grilled, with mozzarella & basil, 93
  porcini mushroom, 92
  radicchio or endive, 92
Roast chicken, orzo-stuffed, & vegetables, 56
Rooster crests with mustard chicken, 57
Rustic lamb spareribs with eggplant sauce, 91

Salads, 19–25
  antipasto pasta, 22
  broccoli, pasta & bean, 25
  crisp won ton, 20
  grilled chicken & pasta primavera, 19
  hot pasta & tuna, 21
  penne with tomato & basil mignonette, 24
  sesame noodle, 24
  stir-fried asparagus & scallops on cool pasta, 21
  summertime pasta, 25
  tortellini, shrimp & pesto, 22
Salmon, smoked, penne with, 47
Sauce
  barbecue, beef-mushroom spaghetti in, 77
  béchamel, 84
  broccoli cream, capellini with, 37
  chicken chili, spaghetti with, 57
  cream, 61, 80
  double mushroom, linguine with, 36
  eggplant, rustic lamb spareribs with, 91
  gjetost, Norwegian meatballs with, 78
  lime-basil, spaghetti squash with, 45
  mint butter, angel hair with shrimp &, 52
  mushroom, barbecued quail with pappardelle in, 73
  mushroom-cheese, tortellini with, 36
  mushroom-tomato, 61
  pine nut–butter, 6
  sweet-sour tomato, pasta & chicken with, 63
  tomato-cheese, wide noodles in, 30
  tomato-onion, 67
  turkey, spaghetti squash, 44
  veal, savory, 45
  veal, zucchini spaghetti with, 45
Saucy chicken & baked polenta, 69
Sausage(s)
  baked polenta &, 69
  Italian, & pasta with basil, 81

Sausage(s) (cont'd)
  pasta &, in Madeira cream, 81
  pistou soup with, 14
  Polish, zucchini & rigatoni, 83
  soup, white bean, pasta &, 14
  -spinach filling, 61
Sautéed liver, green risotto with, 93
Savory veal sauce, 45
Scallops
  & green noodles, 53
  smoked, ginger linguine with, 53
  stir-fried asparagus &, on cool pasta, 21
Seafood, 47–53. See also Crab; Salmon; Scallops; Shrimp; Swordfish; Tuna
Seafood in parchment, 50
Seashells with cauliflower sauce, 28
Sesame
  -lemon dressing, 21
  noodle salad, 24
  seed dressing, 25
Shiitake & cheese cannelloni, 60
Shrimp
  brandied, tricolor pasta with, 52
  & mint butter sauce, angel hair with, 52
  tortellini, & pesto salad, 22
Smoked salmon, penne with, 47
Smoked scallops, ginger linguine with, 53
Soups, 11–17
  chicken-noodle yogurt, 12
  fresh pea & pasta broth, 13
  hoppin' John, 17
  Mediterranean pasta, 17
  pinto bean & pasta, 16
  pistou, with sausage, 14
  ravioli & cabbage, 11
  red bean & lamb, 16
  tortellini, 12
  white bean, pasta & sausage, 14
  winter green minestrone, 13
Spaghetti
  baked tomato, 30
  barbecued crab with, 50
  beef-mushroom, in barbecue sauce, 77
  with chicken chili sauce, 57
  squash, onion-dill, 45
  squash lasagne, 44
  squash with lime-basil sauce, 45
  squash with turkey sauce, 44
  with turkey Parmesan, 67
  zucchini, with veal sauce, 45
Spareribs
  country-style pappardelle, 85
  lamb, rustic, with eggplant sauce, 91
Spicy Mediterranean meatballs, 78
Spinach
  fettuccine, parsley pesto grilled vegetables &, 27
  filling, sausage-, 61
  & garlic, orecchiette with, 39
  -herb pesto, 33
  lasagne with, 77
  pasta, 6
Squash, spaghetti
  lasagne, 44
  with lime-basil sauce, 45
  onion-dill, 45
  with turkey sauce, 44
Star-studded baked pork chops, 83
Stew, garlic veal, & agnolotti, 80
Stir-fried asparagus & scallops on cool pasta, 21
Stir-fried noodles, grilled swordfish with, 49
Stovetop moussaka with green fettuccine, 89
Stove-top polenta, 68
Straw & hay
  pasta, 85
  in tomato cream, 29
Summertime pasta salad, 25
Super-rich fettuccine, 89
Sweet-sour tomato sauce, pasta & chicken with, 63

Swiss chard, pasta with, 34
Swiss cheese casserole, mostaccioli &, 86
Swordfish, grilled, with stir-fried noodles, 49

Tagliarini with chèvre & olives, 41
Tart, polenta cheese, 68
Toasted cabbage with noodles, 42
Tomato
  baked, spaghetti, 30
  -cheese pasta with baked chicken, 55
  -cheese sauce, wide noodles in, 30
  cream, straw & hay in, 29
  dried, pesto, 33
  -onion sauce, 67
  penne with, & basil mignonette, 24
  sauce, mushroom-, 61
  sauce, sweet-sour, pasta & chicken with, 63
Tortellini
  with mushroom-cheese sauce, 36
  & oranges, turkey with, 70
  pasta pie, 84
  pot sticker, 61
  shrimp & pesto salad, 22
  soup, 12
Trenette, baked, with prosciutto & radicchio, 88
Tricolor pasta with brandied shrimp, 52
Tuna
  carbonara, 48
  fresh, puttanesca, 48
  salad, hot pasta &, 21
Turkey
  alla cacciatora, 72
  marinara with perciatelli, 70
  Parmesan, spaghetti with, 67
  pasta, pea pod &, 72
  sauce, spaghetti squash, 44
  with tortellini & oranges, 70

Veal
  green lasagne Donatello, 80
  Norwegian meatballs with gjetost sauce, 78
  pie, Venetian pasta &, 84
  sauce, savory, 45
  sauce, zucchini spaghetti with, 45
  stew, garlic, & agnolotti, 80
Vegetable(s)
  angel hair primavera, 32
  & cheese, 27–45
  lasagne, 39
  orzo-stuffed roast chicken &, 56
  parsley pesto grilled, & spinach fettuccine, 27
  sauce, vermicelli with, 28
Venetian pasta & veal pie, 84
Vermicelli with vegetable sauce, 28

White bean, pasta & sausage soup, 14
Wide noodles in tomato-cheese sauce, 30
Wine-braised chuck roast with bow ties, 76
Winter green minestrone, 13
Won ton
  ravioli, 60
  salad, crisp, 20

Yogurt soup, chicken-noodle, 12

Zucchini
  linguine with, 32
  & rigatoni, Polish sausage, 83
  spaghetti squash lasagne, 44
  spaghetti with veal sauce, 45